THE QUEEN OF SWING

The Willa Mae Lane Saga
1939

BY WILLA MAE LANE

Visit the author's website at: www.willamaelane.com

Publishing Services by Family Star Publishing

ISBN: 978-0-578-32016-8 (Paperback)

Edited by Kimberly Bass Seaton

Printed in the United States of America

Cover & Interior Book Design by Family Star Publishing

TABLE OF CONTENTS

CHAPTER ONE
WHY ME, LORD?

They wheeled me into a room and left me there. Was I dead, or is this a dream? Would I ever hear my name again? "Ladies and gentlemen, the world-famous Cotton Club presents Mr. Lionel Hampton, featuring the beautiful, dynamic Ms. Willa Mae Lane." The thought of never hearing my name again raced through my mind. As I lay here, my face covered with ointment and burning with pain, I cried, "Why me, Lord, why me? My beautiful face, Lord Jesus, why me?" All I could think about was, would I ever see again?

The room was dark, and I was all alone. I could not touch my face, but I could feel my body. I could hear a ringing in my ears and stillness all around me. I could not see, and I just laid there. Why don't they do something? All the pain, someone, please help me, I can't stand it. But I just laid there not knowing what to expect. "Jesus," I screamed, "help me; please, my face is on fire, and my chest is burning." I tried not to pass out because I thought I would die if I did. Why me! I had just come to Buffalo a couple of weeks ago,

working in this town for the first time in a long, long time. The Club Moonglow is a friendly club to work in, and the owners were so lovely to me.

Was I such a lousy person that this should happen to me, and is my career over? I am only twenty-three years old; this can't be happening. I am so young and beautiful. My face was on fire, and nobody did anything about it. My clothes were stuck to my skin where the lye had fallen on my shoulders and chest. I gripped the rail of the bed so tight that my hands were sweating. If I had not, I would have screamed so loud that I would have been heard clear across the country. Don't pass out. Try and stay awake. Just stay awake, Willa, stay awake.

My mind started drifting back to the past to distract me from the pain. I thought about the time I traveled across the country. I thought about Louie Armstrong, who was such a dear friend, and the times we shared and the letters he had written to me. I tried to remember when I first started working with Lionel Hampton and how young I was at the time. I thought about horseback riding with Joe Lewis. He and his wife were so loving to me. My mind was racing, and I thought about everything to take my mind off the pain.

Had I not needed a light bulb for my dressing room, I would have gone straight to the club, and this would not have happened. Had I not cared so much for little children, I would not have stopped to tell them to go home. I thought about all these things. All night I screamed and cried out, "Help me, Lord, help me." This is not fair; it is just not fair, I silently cried, and then I passed out.

I heard a noise that woke me. "Who is it?" I screamed.

"It's your nurse," a voice answered.

"Why don't you do something for me?" I asked her.

She replied, "Until we know something about you, we can't do anything."

"Can you give me something for the pain?" I asked.

"No, I'm sorry, that is against the rules," she said as she left the room.

"Oh, please help me!" I screamed at her, "just go away and don't come back!" I was crying, but there were no tears. "I hate you, I hate this hospital, and I hate everybody in this city." By now, my whole body was on fire. I tried to think about somewhere cold. Was I going to die?!? This can't be happening to me.

I woke to a presence standing above me. "Willa," a voice said, "it's me, Max, Max Levy."

"Is that really you, Mr. Levy?"

"Yes, it's me, and Mrs. Levy is here also. We are here to help you in any way that we can."

"Oh, thank you, God. I am glad that you are here because I do not know what to do."

"Don't you worry about anything," said Mr. Levy. "We'll take care of everything that you need. We'll get you the best doctors and the finest care that we can."

"Oh, thank you, Mr. Levy. I can't see you, so please let me touch you." He reached for my hand, and his touch calmed and reassured me.

Mr. Levy asked, "Willa, how did this happen to you? They told us at the club, but I want to hear it from you."

I began recounting the events to the Levys. "I was on my way to the club when a woman came up behind me and smashed a cup of lye in my face. The cup broke and cut my head. The lye burned my face and body."

"Do you know why she did this?" asked Mr. Levy.

"No, I don't know her. Why would someone want to hurt me?"

"I don't know, Willa, but we'll make sure all your bills are taken care of. We are going to talk to the doctors now, so you get some rest. And God bless you," said Mr. Levy. They left me all alone again with all the frightening thoughts.

I laid there thinking about my eyes, my face – pondering what do I look like. I just wanted to die. What could I do if I was blind for the rest of my life, and what would I do if I was disfigured? I just wanted to die. Time passed, and I didn't know if it was nighttime or daytime. I just laid there in pain. Ella, I thought to myself, where are you when I need you, Ella? I need you, Ella, I cried out. I didn't have any relatives in Buffalo and no close friends except my show business friends. Why did I come to this city? I hate it. I wanted to touch my face, but I couldn't, and the burning pain was making me sick to my stomach. I waited on the Levys to return - not knowing what to do.

If I were a white woman, would they treat me this way? I could hear the doctors and nurses running back and forth, helping everyone but me. I was in a room of the hospital's emergency section, and I couldn't help but wonder, am I not an emergency? I am Willa Mae Lane. I am a star! I have performed for a King. I have been in motion pictures and the star of many shows across the country. And they are treating me like I am a nobody. I started to cry again; what else could I do? I am a colored woman in a white man's world. They don't care about me.

I figured it was morning by now, as I could hear many people outside of my room. Someone asked, "How do you feel? Did you get any rest?"

"I have to have something for the pain. Where is Mr. Levy?" I asked. "I want to see Mr. Levy." I pleaded with them.

A voice said, "I'll see if I can find him for you," and they left. No one is coming, no one. I cried out, "Please help me! Anybody!"

I was crying so hard that I didn't hear anyone enter the room. "Lady Lane, it's me, Jimmy, Jimmy Owens, and Vi is here with me. We came as soon as we heard what happened to you. We are here to help you in any way that we can."

"The news of what happened to you is all over the country," said Vi. "Everybody is in total shock."

"Oh Vi, thank you for coming. I heard a police officer say that they haven't found the person. My face Vi, the doctors said I was blind in my left eye, but they would save my right eye. My face Vi, I don't know about my face. I will never be the same; my life is over. I started to cry, and so did Vi.

"Have faith in God; He will see you through," said Jimmy.

Mr. Levy came back into the room and said, "Willa, we are taking you to the Millard Fillmore Hospital."

"But Mr. Levy, they don't accept colored people in that hospital!"

"They do now; I made sure of that," said Mr. Levy.

"This is Jimmy and Vi Owens, and they are my friends from Cleveland. This is Mr. Levy, my boss. He owns Club Moonglow."

"Jimmy, Vi, will you go with me to the other hospital? I am so afraid to go there after what I've been through here."

"Of course, we will," said Vi. "We are not going to leave you until something is done."

"I've got to go and check on things at the club, but don't you worry about anything," said Mr. Levy.

He left, and the Owens waited for the ambulance to take me to the Millard Fillmore Hospital. "I am so glad you two are here with me. I don't know what I would do if I was all by myself." When we arrived at the hospital, the staff was waiting for me. I had an entire team of people catering to me in a beautiful hospital suite with a living room and bedroom. The Millard Fillmore Hospital was the best in all of Buffalo. My friends Jimmy and Vi stayed with me for a couple of days until my sister Ella got here. I was thankful for them and hated to see them leave, but I knew that they had a club of their own to run in Cleveland.

Ella would be with me for as long as I needed her. After about two weeks, Mr. Levy got the best plastic surgeon in the country, Dr. Brown. He told me, "When I finish, you will be as beautiful as before, and no one will know the difference." I had four operations in all to repair my face. Dr. Brown grafted a new eyelid for my left eye and took hair from my body to make eyebrows. He put my face back together, and he did a beautiful job. I had a little scarring on my body, but you couldn't see it. I thought about my face, but what about my mind. Would my mind ever heal? This brutal act hit me deep in my soul, and I still didn't know who or why someone had done this to me that night.

It wasn't cold that night as I walked along William Ave. on my way to the club. That night, that awful night, I thought to myself. I just went to the hardware store to get a light bulb for my dressing room. After I left the hardware store with the bulb, I saw three little children riding a tricycle, and I said to them, "what are you doing out this late at night? Does your mother know where you are?"

"No, they said. What is your name?" they asked me.

"Oh, you wouldn't know who I am, but your mother might. They call me Lady Lane."

"Can we have some money to buy some ice cream?" the older one asked me.

"Yes, and then I want you to go home - it's late, and I don't want anything to happen to you." I love children so much, and they were so sweet. I bought them the ice cream and told them to go home. They thanked me and started to walk down the street. As they got three or four feet away from me, a woman came up behind me out of nowhere.

I heard her, and as I turned, she smashed a cup into my face. The cup broke, and I felt a burning sensation. I screamed! Then I began yelling, "what have you done to me?" She turned and ran down the street. "Help me," I screamed, "help me!" And people came from everywhere. I called out in painful agony as my skin was melting off my face. "Help me," I cried out, Oh Lord, help me!" I can't get that out of my mind, for it will be with me forever.

After about four or five weeks, I went home, and I had a lot of time thinking and praying. I prayed to my Lord Jesus to help me. I wanted to work again. But since I couldn't get on stage, I had plenty of time to think about my life, family, home on the farm, and traveling across the country and out of the country. I wanted to live a normal life again, but I was not "normal" anymore. I was blind in my left eye, and my right eye was fragile. I knew if the Lord had saved my life, He would let me go back on stage one more time. I started to sing some of the songs I used to sing, "I'll Do Almost Anything for You" and "That's the Glory of Love," then the song "Willow Weep for Me" came to mind, and I started to cry. I wished I had a good man in my life. However, the truth is, I was living a lie with a man I couldn't have. Right now, all I had was time and my dreams.

One night I had a dream that I was flying in the air with angel wings. I had a beautiful costume draped in feathers and a hat with feathers draped across my left eye and around my face. Oh, I could hear music beautiful music, so I jumped out of bed, got a pencil, and sketched that costume. The next day I sent the picture to my dressmaker, Ms. Kate, who lived in New York City. I asked her to make me that costume, for I would soon be back on stage.

I even had thoughts about getting a gun and shooting the woman that threw the lye on me if I could find her, but no one knew where she was. I was afraid to go outside so, I stayed inside most of the time. I would sit and think about her. I was convinced that I would kill her if only I knew who she was. I didn't know, at the time, that it was not me the woman meant to throw the lye on, but another showgirl that was messing with her man. If only they could find her, I would have peace of mind. I used to sit at the window looking at the children playing. One of the little girls whose mother I knew would come by my house and go to the store for me if I needed something. She reminded me of myself.

Figure 1: Willa Mae on stage at the Apollo

CHAPTER TWO
NO COTTON FIELDS FOR ME

I remember running across the fields of our farm. My daddy was a sharecropper, and we had a lot of land. Most of my brothers and sisters worked in the fields, but not me. I just played all the time. We did not go to school, and some of my older brothers and sisters had moved away. I spent most of my days running, dancing, and skipping across the fields, and my mother loved watching me dance around the house.

My siblings did not like me as much as they enjoyed my little sister. They treated her like a little princess. And they looked down on me because I was lighter in skin color than the rest of them. I think they resented the fact that I did not work in the fields.

We did not have toys to play with when I was little, so it was just me and my dreams of becoming a dancer. I often wondered if I was adopted, but I was the only one who looked just like our mother. Most of my siblings were dark, like my father. My parents loved me very much, and I only got one whipping in my life from my daddy. One day my grandmother was sitting on the porch. One of my brothers was making a slapstick out of wood. He sneaked behind her and slapped that stick on the wall, and it made a sound like a pistol. Well, my grandmother thought she had been shot, and she fainted and fell out of her chair onto the porch. My daddy found out, whipped us, and that was the only beaten I got in my life. I was so much like my mother that my brothers and sisters hated me for it, but no matter what, I made up my mind that I would not work in the fields like them. I just wanted to dance, and I knew I was special, and momma wanted the best for me. They hated me for that, and I knew they were always talking about me behind my back.

When I was about eight years old, my brother, Sonny-boy (as we called him), tried to kidnap me for the white man who owned the land my father sharecropped. Most of the landowners in those days would molest and even father children by young girls. If you were light skinned, you were sure to be desired. One day, Sonny-boy tried to get me to go into the woods with him. When I found out what he was trying to do, I started to holler so loud that Sonny-boy got scared and let me go. I turned and ran as fast as I could. Sonny-boy was terrified that I was going to tell my mother about him, but I didn't. I loved Sonny-boy and all of my brothers and sisters and did what I could to protect them at all cost. He tried again, I got away again, and I still did not tell on him. Later, I overheard him tell the white man that he would have to wait a while and try again. That is when I knew I had to get away from here.

When my sister, Ophilla, came home to visit, I told her what happened and that I was afraid to stay there anymore. My big sister convinced my mother to let her take me back to Cincinnati, Ohio. Ophilla told her that she was tired of that white man molesting young black girls. You see, my body was well developed for my age, and I could see how he looked at me. I hated to leave my mother and father, as I loved them very much. I also loved my siblings, even Sonny-boy, but I had to go. Moving to Ohio was going to be a new experience for me, but I was ready to go because I knew that the fields were waiting for me, as I got older.

Ophilla and her husband lived with a wealthy family in Ohio, Mr. and Mrs. Jack Gates. My sister was the maid and cook, and my brother-in-law was the butler and chauffeur. The Gates lived in a beautiful mansion, and my sister and brother-in-law had a whole section of the house to themselves. I was eight years old when I went to live with them. I was so glad to get away from Sonny-boy, the white landowner, and the threat of working the fields.

The people my sister worked for were genuinely nice and they fell in love with me. I used to sing and dance all the time around the house. I did not go to school. So instead, my sister and brother taught me how to read and write, and the Gates would teach me too. Mrs. Gates loved to buy me many pretty clothes and dancing shoes so that I would not scuff up the floors with my regular shoes. They had a big grand piano in the house that they played during their extravagant parties. I became such a good dancer and singer that every time the Gates had a party, I would entertain them, and they had many parties. They would put me on the piano, and I would sing and dance all night for them and their friends. Their friends fell in love with me the first time they saw me. I always had a cute dress on, and Ophilla would fix my hair up nice. She would make me up like a doll.

Living with the Gates was very pleasant. I had a lot of pretty clothes, and I constantly received gifts from many people. Back home in Alabama, there were many of us, and we did not have much. Living with Ophilla, I had my own room, my own things, and some money to spend on unimportant things. Life was so much better living in Ohio that I didn't ever want to go back to the farm. Cleveland was the biggest city I have ever been to, and it had a lot of people and no cotton fields.

Ophilla and my brother-in-law would take me to the park, and we would play baseball with some of my friends. One of my friends, Sara, had an older brother, Clarence, who played in a band. He was cute, and my other friends, Ella Mae and Juanita, liked him. I didn't see them as much as I would have liked because they lived closer to the inner city, and we lived out in the suburb. We had a lot of fun when we were growing up, and I never forgot them.

I didn't have that many birthday parties like kids do now. When my birthday came around, Ophilla and her husband would pack a picnic lunch, and if some of my friends were around, we would go to the park and have a birthday party in the park.

We spent most of the holidays by ourselves. Christmas, we had a white tree upstairs in our part of the house. The Gates also had a white tree in their living room. They didn't have any children, so they never had too much company over, except for parties. Maybe that's why they had so many parties. At Thanksgiving, my sister would cook up many good things to eat. I would help her from time to time, but I tried not to get into a cooking habit. We ate well, for my brother-in-law did all of the shopping for groceries, and whatever he would buy for the Gates to eat, he would buy the same for us.

As I got older, my dancing and singing skills began to advance. Ophilla was strict with me. I partially believe it was because my body was well developed, and so my sister watched me all the time. When I was twelve, I made up my mind that I would not work as a maid or a cook if I could help it. I left home because I did not want to work in the fields. Now I was faced with being a maid or cook. This was not going to be life for me. I dreamed of being a great dancer and singer one day, of taking bows, having my picture taken in pretty costumes, and my name up in lights. I was determined to make it. I wanted to be a great star one day and have a nice car and house. I could see my life the way I wanted it, not how my sister envisioned it to be. Ophilla would be a cook for the rest of her life if she couldn't do anything else and at the same time try to make me into one.

"Dance, dance, dance," my sister would say to me. "That is all you want to do. You are going to wear the floor out, girl. You'd better get over here and help me," she would say to me all the time. I hated doing chores, and I tried to do as little as possible. I could butter up Mrs. Gates to get me out of doing some of my duties. Mrs. Gates would take me downtown and buy me something pretty like a new dress or a pair of shoes. She made sure I had whatever I wanted, and I loved her like a mother. Mrs. Gates fussed over me all the time, making sure I was happy. I always wanted to go to school, but we lived in an all-white neighborhood, and the schools were segregated. Since I could not go to those schools, I focused my mind on dancing and singing.

When I was thirteen, I ran away from home. I went downtown and got a room in a hotel, but Ophilla found me. I don't know how she found me, but she did and took me back home. That night, I ran away again and got another room. I always wore a money belt around my waist that I had made, and I had money on me all the time. I always saved my money, for I knew that one day I was going to leave. I also knew that if I stayed in this hotel, I had to get a job. I found myself always lying about my age. But it was necessary to get a job in a theater to be around all the singers and dancers. After all, that is why I had run away from home to be a dancer. All I could think about was being a famous dancer. My first thought was Ophilla would be looking for me, so I did not tell anybody at work where I was living. My sister lived out in the suburbs, and she did not know where I ran off to this time. She had the police looking for me, so I had to be incredibly careful.

My first job in the theater was as a ticket taker and cashier. I did not like that job because I had to sit all day, and I hated to sit too long. One day I went to the manager and told him I wanted to be an usher. This way, I knew that I would be inside the theater and see a professional show. I would only see a little at a time as a cashier and ticket taker.

I continued to dance and sing in my hotel room, and one night the Watts and Rainbow Show was at the theater. I looked up at the stage and was instantly mesmerized by the dancers and singers performing. The music filled the room, and the lights were flashing – before I knew it, something came over me. My body started moving, and I was dancing down the aisle. I was doing flies, splits, and high kicks. Before I knew it, everyone stopped watching the show and focused on me. The spotlight was on me now, and people started clapping for me. The manager of the theater ran in, grabbed me, and dragged me out of the theater. When the show was over, the show's manager sent one of the girls to ask me if I wanted to join the show. I made my way backstage to see him, and he asked if I knew how to do a time step. I proudly showed him the move, and he personally offered me a position. I told him I'd do anything to be in the show. Then he inquired about my age, and of course, I lied about it. He nodded and told me that they were leaving Sunday and to meet them at the train station.

After the show closed that Sunday, I ran to my hotel room to pack and check out, and without hesitation, I ran all the way to the train station. I was not worried about eating or sleeping because I did not ask him how much money I would make and honestly did not care. All I wanted to do was to dance. I thought about Ophilla, the Gates, and my parents. But this was the beginning of the life that I always dreamed about, and I couldn't let my emotions about leaving deter me. I knew that one day I would become a star, and everybody would be proud of me.

CHAPTER THREE
ALL ABOARD

One of the conductors showed me to the Watts and Rainbow rail car. I got on board and found a seat by the window. I was the only person in the car, and it was very quiet. I sat silently, looking out the window, thinking about my family. My heart was beating extremely fast, and I started to sweat. Am I doing the right thing? Will I become a star? I have prayed for and dreamed all my life about this moment, and now it was here. My heart started beating faster and faster, and I began to cry. Will I ever see my family again? I didn't know where we were going or even if I would like to travel with a roadshow. I just knew that I wanted to dance and become a star. One day they will all be proud of me, and I can help them and maybe help my daddy get his own land.

I looked out the window and could see some of the people from the show hanging around. What will they think of me? Will they like me? Am I good enough? Pull yourself together, I said to myself. Shake that nonsense off, and don't show your age. Stop acting like a little girl and stop crying. I started sweating again and started shaking. I closed my eyes and began to pray.

Dear Lord, I am only a kid, and I will try and be a woman. Please, Lord, keep me safe, guide my life, and help me be a successful dancer and woman. Bless my family and friends. Lord, am I doing the right thing? Am I, Lord? Please help me. Amen.

The train jerked as it started up; I could hear the humming of the engine. I was still the only one in the car and could feel my heart – thump, thump, thump. It felt like it was going to come through my chest walls. I began to wonder, as I looked at all the girls on the platform, when would the others get on? Who will sit next to me? Will they like me? By now, the platform was full of people. A few of the guys were fooling around with some of the girls. Everybody was having a good time laughing and talking, and all of them were sharply dressed. At that moment, I was thankful for all the fancy clothes Mrs. Gates gave to me.

Suddenly, Mr. Watts appeared on the platform, walking extremely fast with a man. They stopped at the steps of the car and greeted all the people. The crowd gathered around Mr. Watts, and he was saying something to them that I could not hear. Then the conductor called out, "All Aboard!" Everybody gathered their bags to board the train. At that moment, I started thinking about what personal details I wanted to reveal to Mr. Watts. I can't tell him my name is King. Ophilla would know how to find me if I became a star under our father's name. One of the guys in the band was playing a tune called *Memory Lane*. That's it, I thought to myself. Lane! I will call myself Willa Mae Lane.

The people were still getting on the train, and Mr. Watts was standing on the platform looking for the last person to get on. "All Aboard," the conductor called out for the last time. Mr. Watts looked up and down the platform for the last time and then nodded to the conductor as he boarded the train. "All Aboard," he confirmed as he closed and locked the doorway. When I heard the lock being secured, I finally felt at ease and softly whispered, "I'm definitely in the show."

The car started to quickly fill up. One of the girls sat down next to me. "Hello, my name is Lula Oile. What's yours?" she asked.

I quietly but confidently answered, "My name is Willa Mae Lane."

Mr. Watts clapped his hands to get everyone's attention. "Listen up, people. We have a new girl with us." He made his way over to me and asked, "What is your name again, honey?"

"Willa Mae Lane," I said.

He nodded his head as he announced, "Everybody, this is Willa Mae Lane. Don't worry, honey, you will get around to meeting everyone soon." He turned and started talking to one of the guys.

Lula asked me if this was my first time traveling. I answered yes and shared with her that this was my first job with a show. "You will get used to the train, and it will become your second home. Are you scared?" she asked me.

"Yea," I told her, trying to disguise just how truly scared I was at that moment.

"You better get some sleep," she advised, "we have a long train ride ahead. You will have to learn to get as much sleep as possible because you will put in a full day of rehearsing and performing."

The train pulled out of the station, and we were finally on our way. I looked at Cincinnati going by me out the window. Goodbye, I said to myself, goodbye! Goodbye Ophilla, goodbye Mrs. Gates, and goodbye to the life they wanted for me.

All of the people in the car seemed so excited - yet relaxed. Some of the musicians were playing a tune. A couple of the girls were dancing a jig. People were chatting, some were laughing, and Mr. Watts was observing it all while puffing on a big cigar. I sat in my seat and tried to relax, but my mind kept racing. Try and get some sleep, I kept telling myself, you have a long day ahead of you. I looked out the window staring into the distance, wondering, am I doing the right thing? Oh God, will I be all right? What if Mr. Watts finds out that I am only thirteen? Will he send me home, and will all the girls laugh at me? What am I going to do? I closed my eyes to try and calm my anxieties. Eventually, I fell asleep.

"Willa, wake up. Wake up, girl!" Lula said as she was shaking me. The train was pulling into a station. I didn't even know where we were. Mr. Watts began shouting out instructions. "Okay, people, let's get a move on it! We have to check into the hotel and then get over to the theater to rehearse. Willa, you go with Lula, and she will show you what to do." Still sleepy and a bit groggy, I nodded in agreement and began moving in the direction of the hotel.

After we settled in our rooms, we went to the theater. Now the butterflies were dancing around in my stomach. I had my tights on, and my dancing shoes tied tightly. Some of the girls were limbering up. Some were doing part of the routine. I looked at what they were doing to see if I could follow them. A piece of cake, I said to myself. Mr. Watts called all the girls to line up together. He turned to me and said, "Willa, you watch the girls do the routine a couple times, and then I want you to do what they're doing. Now let's get on with the show, girls, and get it right! I don't wanna be here all day." He went over to the band and started instructing them.

I watched the girls do their routine a couple of times, and Lula said, "Willa, come over here and get in line." Now the butterflies were moving again. My heart was beating fast, and my legs felt like rubber. I kept repeating to myself with the rhythm of my heart: beat, beat, beat, follow the beat. I got in line and followed the routine, but I kicked higher than the other girls when we got to the kick.

"No, no, no," said the leader. "You have to be in time with us." Beat, beat, beat, kick. Once again, I kicked higher than the other girls. "No, no, no," repeated the leader again, but this time in a more aggravated tone. "Now, let's try this again. Beat, beat, beat, kick. Mr. Watts called the leader over to him, and she said, "we'll have to work with Willa."

"Okay, okay!" hollered Mr. Watts, "you work with her and leave me alone. I have other things to worry about now. That is why you are in charge of the girls."

They worked the show that night, and I watched from the side. I wanted to be out there with them, and I knew my time would come.

My heart filled with the desire to dance. I was the only one standing on the sideline. The crowd loved the show, and the girls took a bow and ran off the stage. I clapped, yelled and jumped up and down for everyone. A chill ran up my spine, and I closed my eyes and saw myself on stage. I was doing a dance number that had the audience standing on their feet. When I finished, they gave me a ten-minute standing ovation. One of the girls in the next act bumped into me as she was going on stage. I then realized that I was not yet a part of the show, but I knew my day would come.

The show was over, and we were back on the train going to the next city. Beat, beat, beat, kick. Beat, beat, beat, kick. I could not get that kick with the rest of the girls to save my life. When I kicked my leg up, I automatically kicked it as high as I could. "No, no, no", said Mr. Watts. He continued on, "Willa, you have to kick the same height as the rest of the girls. You will dance in the show tonight because you know the routine, but you will have to watch your kick."

"Yes, sir," I said to Mr. Watts, "and thank you for letting me go on."

"I knew you would get in because you are a good dancer," said Lula.

That night I was in my costume with the rest of the girls. As we waited to go on stage, the butterflies returned, and I broke out in a cold sweat. This is it, I said to myself. Finally, our music came on, and we ran onto the stage to the spot where we would start our routine. We started our dance number, and I began to relax into the routine. We danced across the stage - beat, beat, beat, kick. Boy, was I out of step with everybody in line. Beat, beat, beat, and kick. Beat, beat, beat, and kick. The audience started to laugh and thought it was part of the show. We went into the next routine and then beat, beat, beat, kick, and they started to laugh again. I felt so out of place, and I knew they were laughing at me. When the show was over, Mr. Watts came over to me and said, "Willa, you are going to have to put in some extra time working on that kick."

"Yes sir," I said and tried to think of what was happening to me, but my mind just went blank. Is he going to fire me? I have to get that kick!

The next night as we lined up to go on, Mr. Watts gave me a strange look as if to say you better get it right. The girls started telling me that I was a good dancer, and I could do that simple little kick. "Come on, girl, you can do it," they said. The band started playing our music, and we ran onto the stage. The routine started, and we danced across the stage. Then it came - beat, beat, beat, kick. Beat, beat, beat, kick. I was out of sync again, and the audience started to laugh, but I could see Mr. Watts was not laughing. I knew that he would fire me now. When the music was over, we ran off the stage. Mr. Watts said to me, "Willa, I am giving you one more chance."

"Oh, thank you, thank you, Mr. Watts."

One of the girls said, "You sure are lucky. Mr. Watts doesn't give too many chances." We left the theatre and went straight to the train and on to the next city.

We had a day off, and I practiced my kick all day. For some reason, my leg wanted to go as high as it could. Some of the girls worked with me. Beat, beat, beat, kick. It was as if a rope was tied to my leg, and someone was pulling on it. Up, up, up - it would pull, but I was determined not to kick so high. On opening night, Mr. Watts put our act on last. I felt this was my last chance. Sure enough, my kick was too high. After the show, Mr. Watts came to me and said, "Willa, you are a good dancer, but you can't keep on going the way you are."

"Let me dance by myself," I asked him.

"Now, Willa, I can't do that. You just started with the show. What will the other girls think?"

"Let me try a number with the girls in line and me dancing on the side?"

"I don't know, said Mr. Watts, "I will have to sleep on it. I'll see you tomorrow". After he left, I started to cry. If he does not let me dance by myself, he will never let me dance in the line again. I have to dance, or I will have to go back to Cincinnati, and I can't do that.

The next day we were on the train again. Mr. Watts didn't say too much to me. When we got to the next city, Mr. Watts called a meeting and told the girls that he was trying something new. When he told them what he would do, some of the girls didn't like it, but they would try anything to keep me in the show. We did the same routine, but I made up another routine to go with them. Mr. Watts liked it and announced that we would try it tonight. To his surprise, the audience liked it too. Now I was where I wanted to be. We worked that show for a couple more cities and was now in the Deep South -- *Mississippi*.

We were in Be-Not, Mississippi. Which meant, be not out after dark. It was a small sundown town – we knew where not to be once the sun set. We had the day off, so a couple of the girls and I went to town to do some shopping. We stopped at a general store to buy some fabric and personal things. Two colored boys came in and started to mess with us. They got loud and started cussing—the lady who owned the store called the sheriff on them. We were scared and didn't know what to do, so we didn't do anything. The two boys ran off when the sheriff arrived. He quickly got out of his car, ran into the store, and drew his gun. He put his weapon upside my head and said, "don't you niggers move!" The lady that owned the store told the sheriff that we were not the ones that were causing the trouble.

"It was a couple of colored boys," she told him. Had it not been for the owner, I am sure that the sheriff would have shot me. When we got back to the train, we told Mr. Hunt, the white man who owned the Watts and Rainbow Show, about what happened to us. Angrily, he went to town to get things straight, but we never went back to town for the rest of our stay in Be-Not, Mississippi. "All Aboard"! Those were the best words I heard.

Now, I was dancing in front of the line, and some girls didn't like it. However, it was too late now because I was the hit of the show. I thought about my sister, Ophilla. If she could see me now. My mother would be so proud of me, and my other siblings would start to like me. One day I will get star billing, I thought to myself, and my name will be in the lights. I've always loved to dream, and now my dreams are coming true. What if I had not been different or if I could not kick as high as I did? I would be in the line – with everyone else - for the rest of my life. What if I was in Alabama on the farm? Would I be picking cotton or having a baby by now? No, no, no! This is what I want to do, and one day, the sign will say, "Willa Mae Lane."

During our spare time, we played cards. We would play Bid Whist, Coon Can, and Pitty Pat. One day we were on the train playing cards on our way to another city, and the conductor came in the car and started to count the people in the car. I got down real low, and the girls put a blanket over me like I was a table and continued to play cards. You see, many times, Mr. Watts would not pay for all the seats, so we had to hide from time to time. When the conductor finished counting, he turned to exit the car and yelled out, "you can come out now!" And then he laughed.

Now we were heading north again. We had played theaters all over the south. I thought about the experience I had. I knew we would be going back to Cincinnati soon, and I would have to be careful. I was sure that Ophilla was still looking for me. We worked shows closer and closer to Cincinnati, and finally, we were back in good ole Cincinnati. I got down real low as we were pulling into the station, but who would be waiting at the station after all this time? It had been about seven months since we left.

We checked into a hotel that day, and I made sure that I did not go out until we were on our way to the theater. We played the Strand Theater that night, and I was very nervous. What if someone who knows me is in the audience, and I am out front now and can't hide? No one in Cincinnati knows that I am with the show. And I am in costume with my face made up. No one will know me. I was standing in the wing waiting for my turn, and I thought to myself, this is the city where my big break to become a dancer began. I remembered that first night when I worked at the Roosevelt Theater. I couldn't help myself and started dancing in the aisle. Boy, was that a funny sight when the manager panicked, ran in, and dragged me out of there! Now, here I am starring with the Watts and Rainbow Show – in Cincinnati.

"Willa, you are on," the stage man called to me. The music started, and I danced on the stage. I was proud to be here in Cincinnati – back home. As I danced across the stage, it was like I was floating on a cloud. My head was up high, and every kick I made confirmed and demonstrated – I was the Queen of the show. I was as graceful as a swan, and the audience stood up and applauded.

On the last night of the show, I danced onto the stage, and as I turned towards the crowd, I saw a police officer standing in the left aisle. I danced to the other side of the stage, turned, and saw Ophilla and another officer standing in the right aisle. Oh my, I thought, what will I do now? I danced and danced and danced, and the band didn't know what was going on. Nevertheless, they played on and on, and I danced on and on - stalling, trying to develop an escape plan. What was I going to do? Now think, girl, think. How are you going to get out of here? I looked to the side of the stage to see if there was another police officer, but it was clear. Now how will I do this? I continued to dance. By now, the band started to play off notes, and then they abruptly stopped playing. What do I do now? I continued to dance and danced right off the stage.

I danced out the door and ran as fast as I could with my costume and dance shoes on. As I was running down the street, I flagged a cab to take me to the hotel. Once there, I packed my bags as fast as I could and changed my clothes. There was a knock at the door. Oh no, they found me. What will I do now? I know; I will go into the next room and down the fire exit. Now they were banging on the door. It is time to go, and through the door, I went. I got another taxicab to the train station. Ophilla was more than likely looking for me at the bus station.

She didn't know we had our own rail car. I waited for the rest of the show to arrive, so we could get on our way. Boy, was I relieved when we left Cincinnati - that was a close call. Ophilla never found me after that.

"All Aboard!" We were on our way to St. Louis now. No one knew what happened in Cincinnati, and I never told anyone. I thought about never going back to Cincinnati until I was grown. This way, Ophilla could not do anything to me. After St. Louis, we went to Chicago to play our dates. Then the show broke up. I joined another show called the May Mac Merry Makers, owned by a man they called Brother Rareback. We headed to Canada, and we worked all the state fairs and theaters in Vancouver and Edmonton and then worked our way back to Chicago. "All Aboard!" This would be the last time I would hear that, for I made up my mind that I would create my own act and work for myself. One-night gigs in whistle-stop towns were starting to get next to me. It was time to get out on my own. Willa Mae Lane would star in the next show she performed in. I will create an act that will have the whole country talking about me.

CHAPTER FOUR
ALL ALONE

After my tour was over, I went back to my hotel room to try and figure out what to do next. I sat there all-night thinking - what do I do now? I looked out the window at the stars in the sky. Lord, what do I do, what do I do? I am thirteen, have traveled across the country, and now I have decided to go out on my own. Now, how do I do that? How do I put together a solo career? I sat back in my chair and closed my eyes. I started to cry for I was all alone. The show was over, and my show family was going home and making other arrangements. I now understood what being alone all was about.

I got up and went to the mirror; I looked at myself and saw my mother's image staring back at me. I imagined she was in the room with me and started talking to her. "Mother, I am so scared; what do I do? I miss you and daddy, I miss seeing your face, holding you, I love you, and I need you now." I started to cry again, and she started comforting me.

"Now, Willa, you said you wanted to be a dancer, now how are you going to be a dancer if all you do is cry?"

"But I don't know what to do!"

She replied in her soft, confident tone, "First, you must stop crying, now wipe your face and look at me." I wiped my face and looked into the mirror. "Now, don't you look better? Look at how pretty you are. You dreamed of being a dancer all your life, and now you have started to dance. Don't you look at me and tell me you don't know what to do. Take a good look at yourself; you are Willa Mae Lane, and don't ever forget it."

I repeated to myself: I am Willa Mae Lane. It seemed that I have always been by myself. I never had a doll or a toy. I rarely had friends to play with. All I did back on the farm was dance and act like a grown-up. Now here I am, a teenager, and I am trying to be a grown-up. Well, I am grown-up.

I wanted to write Ophilla a letter and let her know I was all right. She was the one who taught me how to be a young lady. She taught me to be responsible and how to conduct my life. I can't write Ophilla and tell her what I will do. I am going out on my own, and that is that. I ran myself a tub of water and took a hot bath. I sat in the tub for what seemed like five or six hours, thinking of trying to put it together. I had made many contacts when I was with the Watts and Rainbow Show. I knew what cities were good to work in and which ones were not. I met some of the theater managers, and they liked me. Now, who do I call first, and what type of show do I try to get into? I know that I won't star at first, for I will have to make my mark in the theatrical world. I have to get out there and show them what I can do.

After I finished my bath, I was so excited that I could not go to sleep and started to dance. I closed my eyes and danced around and around. I could see myself on stage at a grand theater with all the lights shining on me, while the audience sat on the edge of their seats in anticipation of my next move. The music played a beat that had me flipping in the air, and I came down into a split. I took my bow as the audience gave me a standing ovation.

I decided to go to bed as I had a long day in front of me. I got down on my knees, and I prayed to God to help me make the right decision, guide my career into the spotlight of life, keep me safe and help me grow. I got into bed, but it was hard to go to sleep. I tossed and turned for half the night and then finally went to sleep.

The sun crept its way into my room through the curtains; as I lay there, I watched it move across the room. I lay there thinking, should I take the first job that comes my way, or should I wait for the right job, one that could help further my career? I had saved my money and had enough to live off for a while. Maybe I will try something new; I had read about a show called the Brown Skin Models. They wore beautiful costumes and played at big theaters. That's it; I will contact the owner of Brown Skins Models! I jumped out of bed, got a pencil, and started to write a telegram to the owner of the show. I checked the paper to see who he was and where they would be performing. I put on my clothes and ran to the Western Union office as fast as I could. After sending the telegram off, I walked back to the hotel thinking about Brown Skin Models. Now to wait until I hear from him.

All that day, I did not know what to do with myself. I paced back and forth, I looked out the window, and I tried to lay down. What if they didn't need another girl? Now wait one minute, I said to myself. When Willa makes up her mind to do something, she does it. The Brown Skin Models will call me in for an audition, and that is that. The day goes by fast when you are waiting for something to happen, and before I knew it, it was nighttime. Then another day passed and another. Finally, a telegram came from Mr. Irvin C. Miller, who owned the Brown Skin Models. The telegram stated that they would be in Philadelphia, Pennsylvania, the following week and if I wanted to audition to be there. Oh, thank you, God, thank you! I was so excited I didn't know what to do with myself. I jumped up and down, crying, singing, dancing, and rejoicing. Oh, thank you, Lord.

After I calmed down, I went over to the train station to buy a ticket to Philadelphia. On my way back, I was dancing and singing up and down the street. People in the street must have thought that I was crazy, for I was flipping, twirling, and doing cartwheels all the way back to the hotel. I was happy that I wanted to shout to the world: Willa Mae Lane will be a Brown Skin Model! I wanted the whole world to know. I returned to my hotel and told the desk clerk that I would be leaving next week and didn't know when I would return. I told him I had a job in Philadelphia, for I know the job was mine.

When I got to Philadelphia, I got a hotel room near the theater where the show was performing. After I got settled, I went to the theater to audition. While waiting to see Mr. Miller, I watched some of the girls as they walked up and down the runaway. All the girls walked as if they were queens, so graceful, elegant, and beautiful. The costumes made the girls look like swans in living color with all the feathers and the beautiful headpieces. The Brown Skin Models were like the Ziegfeld Girls, but with brown skin. Several girls were auditioning. Mr. Miller was sitting in the audience as the stage director called each girl to the stage. He had them walk back and forth. When my turn came, I walked out onto the stage as if I owned the world. I strutted up and down the stage. When I made my final turn, I looked at the stage director and said, "When do I start?" He looked at Mr. Miller and told me to wait with the rest of the girls. He went down to where Mr. Miller was sitting to discuss. They talked for a long time, look up at us, and then started talking some more. I began to sweat a little, but I knew I had a job. Some of the girls were chatting with each other, and I overheard a few saying that they hoped they made it. Finally, the stage director came back up on stage, looked us up and down, and said, "You, you, and you." I was selected. He thanked the rest of the girls and told them that he would get in touch with them if they needed them in the future. He gave us some papers to fill out and told us to report that afternoon for rehearsal.

The three of us were in our dance warm-ups, standing in the side wing of the stage. I looked at all the girls, and they were so beautiful. Am I that beautiful? We watched the girls already in the show performing their routines. Then we joined them on stage. After rehearsal, the stage director told us what time to be at the theater. That night as I stood in the line in my costume, I looked and felt like a goddess. "Ladies and

Gentlemen, the Brown Skin Models." I worked with the show for about three weeks, and then I decided to try to put my own dance routine together. I left the show and worked on my own act; when I thought I was ready, I contacted the Michigan Democrat Club in Detroit, and off I went. Now I was ready to be a star and dance my way to fame and fortune.

When I got to Detroit, I got a room at a hotel. When you work in show business, you live from hotel to hotel. You never get a chance to have an apartment. After I got settled in, I went to the club to check things out. I looked at the billboard, and there was my name, Willa Mae Lane. That was the first time my name was on a billboard as the star of a show, and it felt great. I stared at the billboard, thinking this is my first real break, and I'm going to make it big from now on.

I met all the people that worked at the club, and they were friendly folks. The guys in the band were great musicians. We rehearsed for a couple of hours, and we got in the groove and started to cut up a little. It was great; I felt right at home at the club. After we finished rehearsing and I was leaving, I noticed many tough-looking guys going upstairs over the club. I asked one of the guys in the band what was up there. He told me the champ was up there. Curiously I asked, "The champ? What champ?"

"The champ, Joe Louis, the world's heavyweight champion, his gym is up there," he told me.

"Oh yeah," I said like I knew who he was. I had never seen a boxer in my life.

That night as I was waiting in the wings for one of the other acts to finish, I saw Joe Louis when he arrived. "The champ's here, the champ's here!" Joe had many people with him, and the club provided a big table for him and his party girls. "Does he come to the club a lot?" I asked one of the girls.

"Yes, he comes in all the time. He's a great guy," she told me. I started to get nervous and began to sweat - I was on next. My cue came from the stage director - it was my time to go on. This was my first time on stage as a solo act, and the heavyweight champion of the world was sitting in the audience. The music started to play, and I entered the stage doing splits and flips. The crowd went wild! When I finished, they began shouting, "More, more, more!" So, I danced some more. When I finished this time, I ran off the stage; a guy came up to me to tell me that the champ wanted to meet me.

After I changed my clothes, I went out to meet him. I was so nervous when I got to his table. "Willa Mae Lane, this is Joe Louis," the guy said. "Hello, Willa," Joe said.

"Hello Mr. Louis, I am pleased to meet you," I replied shyly.

"Call me Joe," he said. "You are very talented; I like the way you dance." "Oh, thank you, Mr. Louis."

"Make it Joe, will you?" he asked firmly.

"Yes, sir," I said.

He nodded his head and then invited me to his gym. "When you have time, I want you to come upstairs and see my work."

"Oh yes, I will. Thank you, and good night," I said as I turned to leave.

On my way home, I thought about my first performance as a solo artist. I knew I was a big hit. And thought to myself, I think I am going to like it.

That night in my hotel room, I thought about how lucky I was to meet the champion of the world. But I wanted to meet more people. It gets lonely at night living in a room, city after city, without any family with me—no one to talk to, just a kid out on her own. I thought about Mrs. Gates and her big house, and how much fun I used to have in it. I know they're still looking for me. Ophilla will never give up trying to find me. I took a nice hot bath to relax my body and mind, and afterward, I crawled in bed and instantly went to sleep.

I woke up the next day feeling so good about what had happened last night. To think little ole me meeting Joe Louis. I wanted to open the window and let the world know that I had met the champ. Then I thought about Ophilla. How could I not tell her what is happening to me? After all, she is my best friend as well as my sister. One day soon I will write her and let her know what I am doing. I miss her dearly, but I have to do what I have to do right now.

When I got to the club, I looked up at the gym and thought about going up there after rehearsal. I said hello to everybody in the club, and they told me how great I was last night. That made me feel good. The guys in the band and I had a good rehearsal, and I told them I would see them tonight. I wanted to go upstairs and see Joe, but I was afraid. I have never been to a gym before. I started to leave, and then I thought, oh go ahead, go up there.

When I walked in, I could smell sweat and feet. How can anybody stand this place? I looked at the ring and saw Joe boxing another guy. How can they hit each other like that? When Joe finished the match, he came over to me and said, "you were amazing last night! We will all be at the club again tonight. Will you sing a special song for me?" I blushed at his request and agreed to do so. We said goodbye, and I went back to my hotel room.

But this time, the room didn't feel so lonely. I was singing, dancing, and felt good. I kept thinking, what am I going to sing? The champ wants something special. I sang all the songs I knew, but I didn't know what he liked. This is a new experience to me, I never knew anyone as important as Joe Louis. I sang a couple more songs and got ready for tonight.

The club was packed that night. The Three Rockets were dancing on stage, and people were sitting and standing everywhere. Joe and his party came in, and the audience cheered him. The first act of the night went over big. The crowd was alive and excited. The music was grooving, and the next act was getting ready to go on. I stood there waiting to do my thing, determined to bring the house down tonight.

My music came on, and I danced out onto the stage. The crowd started to applaud. I knew I was going to knock them dead. I did a cartwheel and came down into a split. Boy, oh, boy, here I go! I did a couple of new steps that they loved. I did a few more steps and took a bow. The audience went wild. I stopped to catch my breath. Once the room quieted down, I told the crowd that this song is dedicated to our champ, Joe Louis. I started to sing, "That's the glory of love." When I finished and took my bow, the audience clapped and whistled in approval. Joe sent me a bunch of flowers onto the stage. I took a final bow and ran off the stage to his table. He stood up and applauded my performance. We briefly chatted, and he invited me to come to his home and ride horses with his family. I lied and said that I had never been horseback riding before. He said, "don't worry about it; we will teach you."

The next day we went horseback riding, and our friendship began to blossom. I went on to become good friends with Joe. He treated me like a little sister. We had a lot of good time together. Joe and his wife were very good to me. He had a heart of gold. Joe was well known for being the heavyweight boxing champ and always taking care of people and making sure they had what they needed. He was always giving, and with that smile of his, you knew he was a happy man. The Louis family was my newfound family, and I knew I could call on them for anything I needed or wanted. I spent most of my free time with them and I became a good rider.

After working at the club for a while, I got another job at a theater. I was doubling in a stage show called David and Goliath. I worked at the theater in the daytime and the club at night. After working at the Michigan Democrat Club for about eight months, I met a man named Al Richie. He was a show promoter for the Cotton Club. At the time, he was looking for a show to put in Frank Sabastian Cotton Club in California. Mr. Richie auditioned a lot of us and decided to take me, the Three Rockets, Alberta Pine, Shelton Brooks, Sox Chorus Girls, and Genie LaCort with him. All of us worked at the Michigan Democrat Club or other clubs in Detroit. I hated to leave Detroit because I had made a lot of friends. The people and the owner of the clubs were very kind to me. I was going to miss them; how could I ever forget Joe and his family? He was like a brother to me. He told me to keep in touch with him, and if he was in California, he would look me up. Once again, I was packing and moving, but this was the only way to further my career. California, here I come!

CHAPTER FIVE
A STAR IS BORN

When we arrived in California, we went to the Clark Hotel in Los Angeles. It was fascinating to be where many great entertainers lived. It was a lively establishment—full of dancers, singers, musicians, actors, and comedians. But the Cotton Club was all I could think about. Frank Sebastian's Cotton Club was in Culver City, about five miles from Hollywood. The club was bigger and more fabulous than the one in New York City. Movie stars and people connected with the industry went to the Cotton Club. All the rich and very rich went to the club. You usually only hear about the Cotton Club in New York, but the Los Angeles version was the club of all clubs. Mr. Richie had recruited us from Detroit and created this show to perform at the club. When the word had gotten out that he was trying to put the whole show in the club. However, all the showgirls that worked at the club told Mr. Sabastian that they would strike if the Richie Show came in. That created a problem for us, you see; Mr.

Richie brought all of us to California to be in the show. And we all expected to be working when we arrived. But due to the threat of a strike, Mr. Sabastian told us that he would only be able to use some of us, but we all had to audition for the show the next day. We went back to the hotel, and I could see a look of pure disappointment on everyone's face.

Once in my room, I sat in a chair and looked out the window. This was my first time in California. What am I going to do now? Mr. Richie had all of us come here thinking we had a job. I started to cry. I was all alone and again having to possibly start all over on my own. At that moment, I remembered when I was twelve years old, living with the Gates, and determined that I was not going to be a maid like my sister. I was going to be a star. Now I am in California, fourteen years old, and already an experienced performer. I can't quit now. I am going to get a job at the Cotton Club, and that is that.

The next day, I got up early, got dressed, and went over to the club. But I was not the only early bird. Everyone all arrived well before Mr. Richie was expected. When he arrived, he told us that he would get everybody some work somewhere. The auditions began, and I knew everybody was going to do their best.

Figure 2: Willa Mae Lane at the beautiful
St Michael Bar Room in Ontario, Canada.

The Cotton Club was a performer's dream come true. When my turn came, I gave the band the song, and when I started to dance, I knew I had a job. After everyone took their turn, Mr. Sebastian told us that he would keep the Three Rockets and me. I was so happy I didn't know what to do or say. Mr. Richie told the others that he would help them get into the other show and theater. He knew the people at the Burbank Theater and the Hi Hat Night Club. Eventually, he kept his promise and was able to get everybody a job. But I was going to work at the Cotton Club.

At the time, Les Hite & His Orchestra was the house band at the club. The Three Rockets and I rehearsed with the band. When we finished, they informed us of our lineup order. I went back to the hotel to rest. I lay in bed trying to get some sleep, but all I could do was toss and turn; I couldn't go to sleep. My mind was a million miles away. I thought about when my brother tried to steal me for that white landowner. Now I am getting ready to entertain before some of the wealthiest white people in the country: me, Willa Mae Lane. I wondered what my brother, Sonny-boy, was doing now. If he was trying to get my little sister. I thought about writing my mother to see if the family was all right. I wanted to tell her that I was dancing at the Cotton Club and I was doing fine, but I still couldn't let anyone know where I was.

Although I could not sleep, my mind was at ease, knowing I didn't leave home (Alabama and Ohio) in vain. I was pursuing my dreams and succeeding. That night at the club, the guests were pulling up in big cars and limousines. The doorman was helping the ladies out of their vehicles. They were dressed in beautiful clothes with diamonds and jewels on. Some had on fur coats. It was a star-studded fashion show. I knew that one day I would be wearing similar high-dollar clothes, furs, and jewels. This is my big night, and when I finish, I will be the hit of the show.

I was standing in the wing, looking out at the crowd, and people were everywhere. The club was twice the size of the Cotton Club in New York and was very plush. They had a big dining room, and it was exquisite and had a big bar with tables everywhere. They had another big room for gambling and private parties. I watched one of the other acts waiting on my turn when I looked out into the audience and saw Jimmy Durante and John Wayne. Oh my God, I said to myself. There are real movie stars out there. The Three Rockets went on next, and those boys could dance. When they finished, the crowd went wild. I looked over at Mr. Sebastian standing in the doorway of his office. He looked very pleased with the Three Rockets. Another act went on before me, and I looked over at Mr. Sebastian again. He was always standing in the doorway looking out at everything that was going on in the club.

The music came on for me. I went onto the stage with a beautiful gown on and started to sing the song, "I'm Confessing That I Love You." When I finished, they gave me a standing ovation-I knew I had them now. I looked over at Les Hite, the bandleader, and nodded to him to start my dance number. I had a gown on that snapped together, and I could pull off with one move. The drummer began to play as I began dancing. I danced for about five minutes doing everything I had in my arrangement. I wanted to make sure that when I finished, they would remember Willa Mae Lane. When I finished, I was out of breath, and the audience was on their feet shouting for more. I gave them another number and ran off the stage. I looked over at Mr. Sebastian; he was smiling. I knew I was in now. Backstage, everyone told me my performance was outstanding. Happy tears rolled down my face as they hugged and congratulated me. It was wonderful! Later, Mr. Sebastian told me that I would be at this club for a long time if I kept this up. One of the girls said that if you work out really good, you will get a chance to work the tables after your act and you can make tons of money in tips.

Back at the hotel, I stared out the window, thinking about the day I would be considered a big national star. My dreams were finally coming true, and my family would be proud of me. I couldn't wait for tomorrow to come so that I could go back to work. I took a hot bath and went to bed.

I got up early the following day. The sun was very bright; there was not a cloud in the sky. It was a beautiful day, so I decided to go for a walk. I was looking for a place to rent a bicycle. Riding through the city was one of the ways I stayed in shape. As a dancer, I had to be careful about my weight and keep my body well-tuned. When I was ten years old, Mr. Gates bought my first bicycle. It was a pretty bike, with a fancy seat and basket on it. Ophilla used it to keep me out of trouble. When I would get on her nerves, she would say, "go outside, ride your bike, and don't bother me!" The Gates had a big yard, so there was a lot of room for me to ride. I sure miss that bike. I walked around for a while, unable to find a bicycle rental place, so instead, I decided to walk over to the club and rehearse for the night.

Once inside, it no longer felt like a new place-it felt like I always belonged there. Some of the girls were dancing and the band was playing. As I walked by, many of them said, "nice going," "great act," "knock 'em dead tonight." It made me feel good that I was part of the show.

"Hey, Willa!" one of the guys called out to me. "They wrote about you in the papers." He read, "The Cotton Club has a new singing and dancing sensation, Willa Mae Lane." As I looked at the paper, my heart became full of joy that the newspapers were starting to recognize me. I rehearsed with the band and then went home to get ready for tonight. That night it seemed that the lights were brighter than the night before. People were everywhere. The stars and famous people had come to see me. The word had gotten out, and everyone wanted to see me dance. I stood in the wing, waiting to go on. My heart was beating fast, and I knew I had to do better than last night. What could I do that I didn't do last night? I started to worry. Then I knew what to do, more of my best.

As my music started playing, I danced onto the stage. This time, I started with my dance number. I did a cartwheel into a flip and came down into a split. I rolled over into a turn and got up, and then I did it in reverse. The audience loved it. The place was buzzing, and I could see Mr. Sebastian was smiling again. I cooled the tempo down with a song, and right when I had the audience where I wanted them, I looked over to the band and gave them a nod. The band played a torrid dance number. I was going so fast that I almost danced right out of my shoes. The music stopped, I took a bow, but they wanted more. So, I gave them what they wanted; I started to dance. But this time, I wasn't alone. The infamous George Raft jumped up on the stage and began dancing with me. We danced and danced and when the music stopped, we took a bow together. Willa Mae Lane and George Raft! I will never forget this for as long as I live. He hugged me before going back to his seat. I ran off the stage so excited. "Did you see me, did you see me, did you see me?" I asked everyone in the wing.

"Yes, you were great," they told me, "and the crowd loved you." After the show was over, George Raft treated the whole show to whatever we wanted to eat and drink. We went to the dressing room to change clothes and get ready to go home. I sat in front of the mirror and looked at myself. I began thinking of the girls in the Watts and Rainbow Show. I wondered what they were doing now. Boy, if they could see me now. One of the girls asked me if I was going home. I just sat there, in silence, enjoying the moment. I could have stayed there all night.

For the next couple of weeks, I worked the show so well that Mr. Sebastian asked me to work the tables after my act. This was great for now; I could make some extra money. My friends, Jennie and Shelton Brooks, both lived at the Clark Hotel. Jennie met a guy named Earl Dancer. He told us that we should get a house to live in and move out of the hotel. Jennie and I found a big, elegant place. She even sent for her mother to come live with us so that someone would be there when we were working.

Things were going well now. After my act, Martha and her son, Cliff Richie, and I would work the tables. Working the tables was going to a table and singing for whoever called you over. You would sing and maybe dance a little for them, and they would give you a tip after you finished. I started to make plenty of money working the tables. Some of my favorite customers were Jimmy Durante and George Raft. When John Wayne came in, he would also call me to his table. Jimmy Durante would give me a twenty-dollar tip every time I went to his table. The funny thing about working the tables was that often the customers were so drunk that they would not give you a good tip, but they turned out to be the biggest tippers. When we finished for the night, we would split our tip money with the musicians.

I had one bad experience at the club. One night, after my act, I went over to a table where the cowboy movie star, Tom Mix, was sitting. He stood up right in front of me and scared me. I jumped back, and Mr. Sebastian came running over and grabbed him by the arm to escort him out of the club. Mr. Sebastian was always standing in the doorway looking at everything that was going on. They tell me that Tom Mix was drunk that night, and he didn't like colored people.

By now, I was the star of the show. I had top billing and was riding high. One night I met Cecil B. DeMille after my act. He invited me to his table and told me that he liked what I was doing. We talked for a while, and he asked me if I would entertain at some of his private parties. I was thrilled because he gave some of Hollywood's most fabulous parties.

Jennie's brother, Alfred, and his wife, Hazel, came to live with us. Our family was getting bigger. Jennie's mother, Hattie, took care of us like a mother hen. She started calling me Brown Sugar and I liked it. I was fifteen now, and she was the closest thing I had to a mother. I was still working at the Cotton Club, but Jennie worked at some after-hour club. Her brother was a railroad man while Mamma Hattie took care of the house. One day we decided to get a cook and a maid to help Mamma Hattie with the house. Things went along fine except for the cooking. She would have a habit of not giving us enough food on our plate. Now we paid her and bought the food, but she would put tiny portions of food on the plate like we were birds. I didn't like that cook. We got rid of that cook and got another one, and I let her know about how we liked to eat.

Life was perfect now. I had a new family and was being smothered in love. I never stopped caring for or loving my real family. I often wondered where they were and how they were doing. As my brother and sister got older, some more would get married and move away as life on the farm was not easy.

One day while I was rehearsing, I heard that Lionel Hampton's band would replace Les Hite. Lionel Hampton, I thought. I would love to work with him and his band. He was considered the best drummer in the world at that time. When I do my dance number, I like a drummer that can play with a fast beat and Mr. Hampton was the best.

Working with Lionel was great. He was a master of the drums, but I got tired of working at the Cotton Club. It was the most fabulous club around, but I wanted to move on. It has been over a year since I came to this club, and I wanted to work at another one. I wanted to work with Lionel again, but this contract was not up. He asked me to sing and dance with his band when he goes on tour. This was great for I could work at another club until he got ready to go on tour.

I said my goodbyes to everyone at the club. It was the hardest thing to do, for I was made a star here. Mr. Sebastian told me I could come and work anytime I wanted to at his club. It's not that I was leaving California; I was just going to work at another club. I was getting star billing and could work anywhere.

CHAPTER SIX
JIM CROW MUST GO

I went to work at the Burbank Theatre. Most of the contracts you got in those days would last from four to eight months. So, you had steady work for a long time and could make good money. One thing I learned was to save some money, and I never ran out of it. Some of the guys in the show would be broke and come to me to borrow money because they knew I always had a few extra bucks on me. Things worked out well.

By now, I had let Ophilla know where I was, and she informed me that if I ever needed any money, I could contact her. I would ask her for some money even though I didn't need it from time to time.

I had a run-in with Ralph Cooper at the Burbank Theater, where we worked. Ralph was the producer of the show and didn't like me for some reason. He would always find fault in me, which made me mad, but the people at the theater loved me. Maybe it was because I was the shining star of the show? And to think I got him the job as the show's producer.

One day, Lillian Randolph, a bunch of show people, and I went to a café to get something to eat. Two sailors who were drunk as a skunk came in and started to mess with us, calling us names. Lillian and I thought the guys we were with would do something about it, but they were scared to say anything. So, I told the sailors that they shouldn't talk like that. They laughed and said, "Who's going to stop us, those chicken-little guys you're with?" One of the sailors pulled on Lillian's arm; she grabbed a bottle and hit him on the head. The other sailor was about to jump in when I hit him with a pot I picked up from behind the counter. There we were, the two of us going toe-to-toe with them fighting all over the place. We thought the rest of the gang would help us. But they ran to the back of the café thinking they could escape through the back door, only to find out they couldn't. By now, Lillian and I were beating those sailors to a pulp. I would hit one on the head and spin him around toward Lillian to hit him, then she would hit the other one and spin him around, and I would hit him. Now, they were bleeding from the head, but we kept popping them with pots we had picked up. They were so drunk that they didn't feel a thing but knew they had been in a fight. The shore patrol came in and after we told them what happened, they arrested the two sailors and took them away. All the others came out from the back and started praising us and calling Lillian - Joe Louis and me - Max Baer.

On the way back to the theatre, I thought about Joe Louis and how nervous I was the first time I met him that night at the Michigan Democrat Club. He never knew how old I was, and he treated me like an adult, but I think he knew I was a teenager. Sometimes when we were all together, I acted like a kid. My birthday has come and gone in the past three years and I had let no one know when.

After working at the club that night, I took a long walk back to my hotel room, thinking about my young life. I thought about how I changed from a little girl to a working showgirl in a club where grown people came to see me perform. As I walked alone, I looked up at the sky and gazed at all the stars. One of them was my special star. I knew the good Lord was watching over me with a shining star as my guide.

I thought about my birthday again and the little girl in me came out. I wanted some of the things that teenage girls wanted, like a birthday party. I started remembering all the birthdays I celebrated with my family. I missed them all. I didn't know if they were all right or not. I began to feel really lonely.

Once I was back in my room, I thought about the events of the day, and it made me a little tense. That fight with the sailors was something. I went over to the mirror, put up my dukes, and jumped around like I was a fighter. Left, right, left, right, jab, jab, hook, boy was I something! I jumped around some more, right, left, right, hook, a knockout! "Go to your corner," the referee said and he started to count, "One, two-nine, ten, and you are OUT! The new champion of the world, Willa – Mae- Lane." I threw up my hands and took a bow. Boy, was I some-thing!

I was a little sore, so I took a nice hot bath. While I was sitting in the tub, I started to think about my family again. Was Ophilla all right? It had been almost four years now that I have been gone. I wondered how the Gates were doing. I knew by now that they have seen my picture in the paper. I have been getting plenty of press coverage and my name is in all the show business papers. How many Willa Maes who love to sing and dance are there? They have to know that it's me, I told Ophilla not to tell anybody, but there is no stopping me now.

The next day when I went to the club, all the people knew what happened with the sailors. Lillian and I were the hit of the club. Joe Louis and Max Baer, champs of the day. We got a little ribbing for a while about the fight, but then it died down. My dancing act was so good that I was getting offers to dance at all the clubs. I would finish my contract at the Burbank Theater and move on to another club.

It seems that when you are working in show business that all you do is move on. My first relocation is when Ophilla took me to Cincinnati. Now all I do is move, but that is what I wanted, and I won't stop until I reach the top.

The next club I went to work at was the Hi Hat Night Club. It was a high-spirited club. Livelier than some of the other clubs I worked at, with many friendly people and management. Maybe that's why they called it the Hi Hat Night Club.

After being at the club a while, a casting call for singers and dancers was announced. I thought to myself how wonderful it would be if I could land a job in a movie. I inquired about the film and found out that the stars were Al Jolson and Cab Calloway. Now I wanted to be in it more than anything. I made a good name for myself while working at the different clubs and theaters and knew I could handle anything that would come my way. I made up my mind that I would go and audition for the part the next day.

That night after working the Hi Hat, I went home and told Mamma Hattie and everybody at the house what I would do. They were all overly excited about it. They talked about seeing me up on the screen. Can you see me, Willa Mae Lane, on the picture screen? I told them I am not playing a maid, but a singer or dancer with the great Al Jolson and Cab Calloway.

I tried to go to sleep that night, but the thought of being in a movie kept me tossing and turning all night. I finally went to sleep after half the night had passed. When the sun came up that morning, I jumped out of bed, went to the mirror, looked at myself, and said, "A star is born." I took a bath and got dressed as fast as I could. I said goodbye to everyone in the house and rushed out to the studio where casting was taking place.

On the way to the studio, I thought about when I was a little girl dreaming about becoming a star. At this point, I was seventeen years old, had starred on stage singing and dancing for the past three years in various states. And I was about to get a chance to be in the movies where people that have not seen me on stage will get a chance to see me on screen.

I thought about my mother and father and how they would react to see me, for by now, my whole family knew I was in show business. I was claiming my part in the movie. Oh, how my sister, Ophilla, would be proud of me. And the Gates bought my first pair of dancing shoes and encouraged me to sing for them at all their parties. I can't wait to get to that studio and show what Willa Mae Lane is all about.

When I arrived at the studio, there were thousands of people there. It looked like a circus of people moving about, other people directing people where to go. Some people were just waiting to see what was going on. I asked someone who seemed to know what was going on where I needed to audition for a part. He pointed to where a group of colored people were standing around waiting to be called.

When I got over there and signed in, there were a couple hundred colored singers and dancers there. It seemed like every colored singer and dancer in the country wanted to be in this movie. I didn't see Al Jolson or Cab Calloway anywhere. None of the big stars were at the lot that day, just the people trying out for different parts in the movie.

I was a little nervous at first, but I knew that I could both sing and dance, and they had a big cast in musical movies in those days. The name of the film was "The Singing Kid" starring Al Jolson or Cab Calloway. Boy was this exciting. I worked at the Cotton Club performing in front of these movie stars, dancing and singing, and now I was about to work with them. It was an exciting day for me, one that I will never forget as long as I live.

The other dancers and singers were being called in a couple at a time. You would tell them what you would do, sing or dance and tell them where if you worked at a club or theatre. I recognized several people from working around town and the country; many of them knew me too.

When I got my call to perform, many people came to see me, which made me feel good for a lot of movie people had seen me at the Cotton Club and some of the other clubs around town. I danced and sang for them and when I had finished, they told me to wait with a group of singers and dancers. I knew then that I had a job. Some of the people they just thanked and told them they would be in touch with them if they needed them. I knew they would make another cut, but I was not worried, for I had claimed my job before I auditioned.

After they went through all nine of the contestants, they looked at us again. Finally, I was informed that I would be in the cast and given the details about rehearsal and shooting. I was so excited that I almost screamed aloud. I was screaming inside and busting at the seams. All of us were smiling and very happy for a colored performer didn't get much work in movies, which was a big moment for us.

After filming started, I continued to work at the Hi Hat Club at night while working on the movie set in the day. It was very exciting on the set; after we would do our songs and dance numbers, we could wait around and see the movie stars doing their parts.

The first time Mr. Jolson came onto the set, the crowd got hushed. He was a famous star known all over the world. Al Jolson was best known for his singing and the black face he put on for his act. In those days, that was his way of getting over something different. People tried to make it racial and it might have been, but this was his way of getting over.

The movie had an extensive cast of actors, including supporting people and extras. There was never a dull moment on the set and there were always parties. Some parties we could go to and some we couldn't, but it was great to be there and be on the movie set. I thought to myself, maybe one day I might star in a movie. I am beautiful and talented, and people love me. I am a star of night clubs why not be a star of the movies?

One night after working all day on the movie set and working at the club. I told them we could sue the owner of the diner for not serving us. The rest of the girls were afraid to do anything, but not Marie Dixson and me. That night after I finished working and I was at home, I was mad at the world for what had happened to me. I thought about when I lived in Alabama and we couldn't go in certain places. And the restrooms and water fountains marked COLORED. I didn't understand what was going on in those days because I was a little girl and all I knew was not to use the one marked WHITES ONLY.

When I traveled with the Watts and Rainbow Show, we traveled all over the south and performed for white people. We had to get our food out of the back door of restaurants and couldn't sleep in a hotel of our choice. Years later, I am in Burbank, California and I can't get a meal at a little old diner? Now that made me hopping mad! I got something to eat, took a hot bath, and went to bed. In the morning, I was to going to find a lawyer and do something about what had happened to us.

The following day, I found a lawyer named Taylor. He was one of the best colored lawyers in California. After we talked about what happened to us at the diner he told us how unusual this case was, and he would handle it if we wanted him to. Marie and I were determined to do something about it to prevent it from happening to anyone else in

California. We did not want to be crusaders; we just wanted to have the right to eat where we wanted.

We finished making the movie and I was through with my contract at the Hi Hat Club. Before our case came to court, Lionel Hampton was ready to go on the road. I had been waiting a long time to work with Lionel as his featured singer. I was excited about going on tour with him. No sooner did I go on tour with him, our case called. Mr. Taylor, our lawyer, worked it out where I didn't have to be there. He got a power of attorney from me and Marie would be there to represent us.

After the trial started, the people who owned the diner got together a bunch of people to testify they did not discriminate against colored people. They lied, said that they were there that night, and did not hear them say that they would not serve us. They even got a colored porter that worked there to say that they always served colored people. When our lawyer asked them about the night in question, they said it didn't happen the way we told it. Mr. Taylor's summation, along with my statement and Marie's testimony, proved to be too much for the diner's lawyer. The judge awarded us the victory in the case, and we received one hundred dollars as a settlement. The money was not a significant factor as much as the principle in the matter. After that, colored people could eat in any diner they wanted. Now, there were still restaurants we didn't go into, but we knew that it would not be a problem if we wanted to.

The next day, the newspaper headline read, "Willa Mae Lane Wins Jim Crow Lawsuit." Who would have thought that I, Willa Mae King, from

Clayton, Alabama would be involved in a lawsuit against a white person and win? If the white landowners in Clayton knew it was me that had caused trouble for a white person, they might cause my people problems.

In those days, they didn't pay much attention to things like this because they didn't want other colored people to react like I did and cause more trouble for them. You see, discrimination was not just in the south; it was everywhere.

CHAPTER SEVEN
ON THE ROAD WITH LIONEL HAMPTON

Finally, I became a member of Lionel's Big Band member. We played clubs like Frank Sebastian's Cotton Club. Frank loved my act, but now that I was with Lionel, I was at the top.

He was well-known as "the fastest drummer" in the world. What a title, huh? And he deserved it. Lionel was a good person, friend, and mentor. And so, we now traveled towards the East, playing clubs as we go. It was a great time for such a fantastic act and me. He would start the show by playing a tune on his vibes, then as the music progressed, he would switch over to his drum set, moving his drum sticks around like a machine. Round and round, then he would jump up on his floor drum and start tap dancing. The people would go crazy applauding, screaming, and yelling. Everyone loved Lionel from the East coast to the West coast. Then it was my turn to sing and dance and I loved a tune called, "My Heart Belongs to Daddy". As my song progressed, he would start his fantastic drumbeats. And I would perform my routine of high kicks and flips. The people loved us.

We traveled to New York City, "Home of the Big Lights". I loved New York. It was a great city and time to be an entertainer. Lionel's wife, Gladys, was a beautiful person; she always looked out for me. Gladys was a costume designer and dressmaker. She worked for some of the other stars in Hollywood, including Joan Crawford. One time, Gladys went to see Ms. Crawford and asked me to go with her. I was thrilled and excited! I was going to Beverly Hills to her mansion, and we didn't have to go in through the back door. When Gladys introduced me to Ms. Crawford, she knew who I was and gave me a pair of earrings. I was very honored that she would think of me that way. She told me I was a great performer, and she had seen me at several places.

Figure 3: Willa Mae Lane custom design costume for
performance with Lionel Hampton.

This is great, I thought to myself. I performed for stars and had the opportunity to be in a movie with them, and now I am at Joan Crawford's house with a pair of her earrings on. I wonder what my childhood girlfriend, Sara, would say if she knew that, I was at Joan Crawford's house.

Sara was one of my best friends. When I lived in Cincinnati, Sara, Ella Mae, Juanita, and I played together all the time. Sara had a brother, Clarence, who played in a band at the Ritz Ballroom. We would sneak in the ballroom with Sara. She was a little older than us, but we all looked older than we were. The Ritz Ballroom would have dance contests all the time. Fletcher Henderson was the house band at the time. Little did I know that I would later in life meet up with him. I would enter into every dance contest I could and win. I was a great dancer, and no one could beat me. The first prize was five dollars. The second was three dollars and the third was two dollars. I never worried about the second or third place as I was going to get first. Five dollars was a lot of money in those days, and with a depression going on, I could do a lot with my money.

After working with Lionel for a while, I met a producer, Milton Shouster. He wanted me to come East and work at some of the clubs in Chicago and New York. I was having a good time with Lionel and Gladys, but it was time for me to get top billing and create a new show routine for myself. I talked it over with Lionel, and he agreed I should go out on my own, but he didn't want to see me go.

It was hard to say goodbye to the Hamptons and all the guys in the band as we were one big, and I mean big, happy family. I was going to miss them, but deep down inside, something said you have to go. I thought to myself, where would I get a great band like this backing me up? But I knew I would get with a great band again and be happy. When you work the circuit, you work by yourself for a while with a house band. And you work a bit with a big-name band, and in those days, there were many bands. I had my own car, a convertible, and decided to drive across the country and take my time. I wanted to see my friends in Detroit, but I would stop in Chicago to see my good friends, the Berry Brothers. So, after a long stay in California, I head East. I was leaving good friends and band, my house, my best friend, Jennie, who was like a sister, and Mamma Hattie, who was like a mother.

I drove through California with my car top-down as the sun baked me into a golden-brown color. I thought about all the people that I was leaving behind, and I started to cry. I had such a good time there and got my first big break at the Cotton Club. With tears in my eyes, I thought about how many families I had at this point in my life. Everywhere I worked and stayed, I developed deep friendships and family bonds. Now once again, I was leaving on my own.

I began thinking about Ophilla and her husband and the parties they would have when Mr. and Mrs. Gates would go out of town. It was funny because all their friends were maids and butlers, cooks, and chauffeurs. When they had a party, limousines would be parked everywhere. The neighbors would think that the Gates were having another party because they gave so many. My sister's friends would come in their maid and butler uniforms, and the neighbors would think they had come to work. Little did they know that they were partygoers. In the mansion, they would have fun serving one another. The same as they would at parties for their employers. May I get you something, madam; they would say to one another and lift their pinky fingers in the air as they held a glass up.

When I reached Chicago, I called the Berry Brothers to let them know I was in town. I had just unpacked my bags when they told me they were going over to the Grand Terrace nightclub to see the twelve o'clock show and wanted me to go with them. Before I could say anything, they said they would be right over to pick me up.

People in show business always go see other performers when they have time off. Fletcher Henderson was the house band at the club and Billie Holiday was the singer. The club was a beautiful place and the people were very warm. Billie Holiday sang those love songs with the Blues in them. The ones that made you think about your lover. I didn't have a lover at the time, I was still young, and all I wanted to do was sing and dance. Men were not in my plans back then.

Fletcher Henderson came over to speak, and he asked us to do a number for him and the audience. When you are a performer and stop by a club, they always ask you to do a number for them. The Berry Brothers got up first; boy, could they do the jitterbug jive. They had the crowd jumping with them, boy oh boy, could they dance. When they finished, they got a standing ovation.

Now it was my turn, and I sang, "I'll Do Almost Anything For You". Then I told Fletcher to "hit it", and the drummer started beating fast as I took off doing one of my dance routines. I was flipping and splitting, and the crowd went wild. I was able to do all this with a skirt and high heel shoes on. I always danced in high heels, they loved it and wanted more, but I was not the star there and didn't want to cause any trouble.

After I finished, Mr. Ed Fox, the club owner, came over to me and said he wanted me to work for him and replace Billie Holiday. He told me he liked my act better than Billie's. I told him, "I can't do that, and besides, I am on vacation."

He asked, "How long will you be on vacation?"

"I'm heading to Detroit for a week and then I might be ready to work, but I can't have you fire Ms. Holiday for me. I would not want someone to do that to me. And besides, I don't sing the songs that Billie sings; I sing up-tempo songs."

He told me, "That is what I like, and your dancing too!" He continued, "What if I pay for my vacation and come back and work at the club next week? I'll let Ms. Holiday work this week and pay her not to work the last week of her contract. Does that work, Willa?"

"Okay, yes, as long as Billie doesn't lose any money." So we agreed. Think of that, me replacing Billie Holiday. Boy, oh boy!

I went to Detroit and saw all my friends at the Michigan Democrat Club and at Joe's boxing gym. I had a good time with Joe; we talked about what I have been doing in California at the Cotton Club, making a movie, and about the Jim Crow lawsuit. Joe shared with me that being a heavyweight champion of the world didn't mean he could go anywhere either. People still made colored people stay in their place.

We went horseback riding, and I remembered the first time I told Joe that I had not been on a horse. I only did it so that he would show me some attention, but I had been riding horses for a long time back in Cincinnati. My sister and I rode all the time—Mrs. Gates bought my first riding outfit. I was so cute in it, and it made me feel like a big-time rider. Joe and I had so much fun together, and I hated to leave, but I told Mr. Fox I would be back in time to start the second week of Ms. Holiday's contract.

When I returned to Chicago, I got a room in the hotel. I thought about this new opportunity. How could I replace a singer like Billie Holiday? Someone who sings love songs that touch your heart and makes you reminiscence about your loved one. Now, that's what people want to hear. I am an up-tempo singer and a jitterbug jive dancer.

All this worrying kept me up for half the night. To put on a show that will make people forget about Billie Holiday will be hard to do, but that is why I am here. When I got to the club, I met Sammy Dyes, who produces the shows at the Grand Terrace. We talked about song and dance numbers and about me replacing Billie. I had an uneasy feeling, but he said, "If Mr. Fox likes you, you must be great." The Grand Terrance was one of the top clubs in Chicago. Working with Fletcher Henderson will be as great as working with Lionel Hampton, except this time, I am the star.

I finished talking with Sammy and went over to Mr. Fletcher to rehearse my number. I sang a few songs that I wanted to sing that night, and then I got off into my dance number. If I wanted the people to forget Billie Holiday, it had to be through my dancing because I could not out-sing Billie. But no one could out-dance me; I was the best.

That night, I was a little nervous, not like the night I did a stand-in number. This was my night. I could feel the crowd's energy and, I knew some of them wanted to see Billie Holiday, but they got me instead. When I finish with them, they will know who Willa Mae Lane is and will never forget the first time they saw me. I was ready to put on the best show of my life.

The music came on, and the announcer said, "Ladies and Gentlemen, the Grand Terrance Nightclub proudly presents the Beautiful, the Dynamic Ms. Willa Mae Lane." The audience clapped for me. I came out onto the stage in a dress that held them breathless. The one thing I definitely had on Billie was a body. I sang some of the songs that I knew would please them, and it worked. I looked over to where Mr. Fox was sitting and could tell he was happy with his decision to hire me. I went through a series of songs; I had the audience right where I wanted them. I looked at Fletcher and gave him a cue. My dress was one of my snap-off dresses. I snatched it off in front of them. The drummer started to beat his Tom-tom drum, and I took off dancing across the stage. I did one of my dance numbers that the band, not even Fletcher, had seen. I did another number in rehearsal to the same music, but I switched it up because I wanted everyone in the place to see Willa Mae Lane at her best for the first time.

The audience was standing on their feet when I finished, going wild, and hollering for more. It was at that moment that I knew how good I was. I definitely outdid myself. I told Fletcher to give me another number, and this time I did the one we rehearsed with the band. At this point, the audience just wanted me to dance.

I finished and took a bow, but they still wanted more. They were sending me roses up to the stage. My arms were filled with beautiful bouquets, and they kept them coming. I sang one more song to end the act that I knew would settle them down. I took my bow and the applause lasted for about fifteen minutes. I was a big hit, and I knew they would be back to see me again.

Once I was backstage, everybody came over to me and said how good I was. The crowd outside was still buzzing and wanted more. Mr. Fox came over to me and said how great I was and assured me I would be at this club for a long time. Sammy Dye gave me his nod of approval and I felt great about that. During my time at the club, I continued to pack it, and the people loved me. My dancing was what the people loved the most. Not too many dancers could do the steps I used in my act. When I worked at the Cotton Club, I learned how to get the audience's attention and keep them where I wanted them.

I danced so much that my feet would swell up. After a while, this became a problem. I continued to work through the pain because I loved dancing. I thought that if I soaked them at night and stayed off them in the day as much as possible, the pain would go away. One day my feet were hurting so bad that Davie Jobe told Mr. Fox what was happening to me. Mr. Fox asked me if I had a problem with my feet. I told him it was not bad. It's just that I always danced in high heels and my feet were a little sore.

I tried to hide the fact that my feet were killing me all the time. But I didn't want to stop working. The problem with my feet became a real problem and I couldn't take it much longer. Mr. Fox made me an appointment to see a foot doctor, and he took me there to make sure that

I went. The doctor told me that I had gout in my big toe. I had done a lot of dancing in my young career. The doctor started treating my feet, and before long, they were like new again.

I worked at the Grand Terrance for about six months. When I was about to leave and start working somewhere else, I met Louis Armstrong, who was coming to the Grand Terrace to see me perform. Another girl named Elma Turner, who worked in the show, introduced me to him. He told me he had heard a lot about me and would like to see me someday.

Louis told me that when I finished working here to consider coming to New York and see him. I thought this man is married, but a voice said he's the great Louis Armstrong, so what if he is married? He must like you to ask you to come to New York. He gave me his agent's number and said to get in touch with him when I was ready to visit. I told him I would, and we said goodbye.

That night in my room, I thought all about all the things going on in my life. I was eighteen years old and had never had a man in my life, and here I was with a man as great as Louis Armstrong that wanted me. I thought to myself, what should I do? Now how do I get out of this, or do I want to get out of this? I kept thinking about his wife. What would she think if she knew he wanted me? I was so naïve and young when it came to men. I told him that I would come to New York, but you can't do that. But you told him you would. I wrestled with that all night, and when the morning came, I decided that I would go to New York to see him.

I closed at the Grand Terrace that week. Once again, saying goodbye was difficult to do. When you are in show business, you make a new family everywhere you go, only to leave them after a while and move on to your next show business family.

Mr. Fox and his wife had been so nice to me, and the people that worked at the club were sad to see me go. But go, I must, but this time for another reason. Louis had given me his agent's number in New York to contact him, and he told me that some arrangements would be made for me so that I wouldn't have to worry about anything.

CHAPTER EIGHT
SATCHMO

I left Chicago and headed east to New York. I had one thing on my mind, Louis Armstrong. This man had swept me off my feet in just one meeting. How am I going to handle it, or would I be able to handle it? The sun was bright as I was driving, I had my top-down, and the sun danced across my face. There was a smile on it, thinking about meeting up with a man who was one of the famous-colored stars of those days.

When I got to New York, Louis had a suite for me at the Braddock Hotel in Harlem. In that day, the Braddock and the Theresa Hotels were two of the finest in Harlem. Most of the hotels were designed like small apartments. He had flowers in the room, and he instructed the hotel staff to do or get anything I wanted.

Harlem was different than any city I had visited. It had more colored people than I had ever seen in one place at one time. There were a lot of poor colored there. Colored people had just started moving into Harlem in large numbers after the depression. I could look out my window and see people everywhere, children playing, and old men sitting on the steps of buildings. Some winos were laying in the gutter, and men were pushing crafts, selling fruit and ice. Yes, Harlem was a place like no other in the country.

After I got settled in, I was to meet Louis at the Strand Theatre that night. I thought about what I would say to him, how I would act, and if my actual age would show. Everybody thought I was much older than I was. My entire young career in show business, I told people I was much older than I was. Here I am about to encounter a relationship with a man for the first time, and I didn't know what to do. I started to sweat a little as I thought about what kind of man Louis Armstrong would be once I got to know him. Is he a nice man, is he kind and gentle, or is he mean? All I knew was he was a great trumpet player. As a man, I knew little about him for all this happened so quickly.

I got a taxicab to go downtown to the Strand Theatre on Broadway. Louis was appearing at all the big-name clubs and theatres in New York and all over the country. I played some big-name clubs and theatres too, but not the same circuit as Louis. The people loved to hear him blow his horn and sing in that gravel voice of his. His handkerchief was as famous as he and his horn. The three of them would have the audience on their feet wherever we went. From that day on, Louis and I became close friends.

I fell in love with Louis from the beginning. He was very good to me - a kind and generous man. There was nothing that he wouldn't do or buy for me. He loved to surprise me with gifts. I remember the time he bought me a diamond ring. It was a beautiful ring sparkling with diamonds and in a beautiful setting. That ring was very special.

When I was working in Atlantic City, my mind would be on him; the thought of loving a man that I couldn't have hurt me to my heart, but I couldn't stop loving him, and I knew he loved me. I got to see Louis only when I was not working or when he was in between gigs. Our jobs always put us in different parts of the country, but we always found time for each other no matter how little.

Louis was always arranging for me to be with him after I finished my working assignment. One time I met him in New York when he was working at the Zanza Bar Club on 42nd Street. The Zanza Bar Club was the old Cotton Club. I went backstage to see him, and he had a silver fox coat for me. It was beautiful, long, and very warm. Not too many colored women had fur coats in those days, and I felt lucky to have a man like Louis in my life even though he was married.

We spent a lot of quiet time together. He loved to take long walks and talk about everything. He always told me that he didn't want me to smoke. He didn't like women that smoked, and I didn't smoke. Sometimes we would get into his car and drive to the park. We would walk for miles in the park holding hands like two young lovers. In the beginning, I was just his lover on the side and didn't know where I stood in his life. As time went on, we got closer and closer. He made certain that I was with him when I was not working, no matter what city he was working in. Hotel rooms were always waiting for me with flowers and some wine or scotch in them. We spent a lot of time together walking and talking, then we would go back to my hotel room. There were times when he stayed all night and times when he went home. But I knew that if I wanted him, he would be there.

One time I went to visit him in Rochester, New York, where he was working. He had seen a suit in a store window and told me when he saw it he said, "That looks like Brown Sugar." I loved to hear him call me that, for I knew that this man loved me. When I got to the club that night and went backstage, he said, "Brown Sugar, I saw a suit downtown in a store window that looks like it would be perfect for you. After the show, I will take you downtown and show it to you, but I am not saying I am going to buy it for you, I just want you to see it."

He laughed, and I told him, "if you're not going to buy it, then don't show it to me." He took me downtown showed me a gray wool suit with a Persian lamb collar on it.

"Do you like it baby?"

I said, "I love it, and I love you." The next day he bought me that suit. I had a red silk blouse with a Russian collar made to go with it. Louis was very good to me, always making me happy and always buying me things. He made sure that my rent was always paid, and I had money in my pocket.

As time went on, I found out that Louis liked more women than just me. In fact, he fancied several women. I loved him but could never see myself married to him. I was a one-man woman. He never stopped being good to me and never stopped loving me. It's just that he chose other women as well. That was the type of man he was, and no one could change him.

His wife knew about me and filed for a divorce. She named me in it, and it became very sticky. He told me that after the divorce was final, he wanted to marry me. I thought about it, but I wasn't sure I could marry a man like him. He was very good to me, and I loved him, but he also loved other women. I was already the other woman and didn't want to be the wife who knew that he had other women in his life. I was the other woman now and already had other women to deal with.

I was working in Cleveland when I received the divorce paper for me to sign. I was the third party in the divorce and had to sign. When they first came, I looked at them for a long time, wondering what to do. I had never been in a situation like this before and didn't know how to handle it. I was still just a young woman and didn't have much experience in life to recognize if I had done the right thing. This was one time in my life that I wished I had a close friend to talk to. After he got his divorce, we got engaged for a while, but I knew that he had other women on the side. I knew I could never marry a man like Louis. I wanted a man that only wanted me. And I was certain that if I ever found a good man, I would be through with Louis.

I stayed in Louis' life until I met my husband, Harvey Whited. Louis and I remained good friends after I was married, but I never saw him on the side. Harvey and I would go to see him at different clubs, which was all it was going to be.

Figure 4: Louis Armstrong "SACHMO"

CHAPTER NINE
COMING OF AGE

The headlines read, "Willa Mae Lane tops the new Sepia showpiece at the Cedar Gardens with her torrid dance number." Oh, boy, do I remember Cleveland and working at the Cedar Gardens. It was a fabulous club, one of Cleveland's finest. I was starting to stretch out now, working at all the fine nightspots. The newspapers would follow me everywhere I went. My name was always up in lights and cameras, always taking my picture. Life was beautiful for me, and to think this is the same Willa Mae King who ran away at the age of thirteen to chase a dream.

By now all my family knew what I was doing. My sister, Ophilla, my best friend in Cincinnati when I was growing up, was very proud of me. I remembered when Ophilla worked at the YWCA as a part-time guard and swimming instructor. She tried to teach me how to swim, but I never got the hang of it. I loved to play in the water and just hang out around the pool. At the "Y" I got a chance to play with a lot of girls my age. We played checkers, cards, and any of the games that they had. There were books to read, and Ophilla and I would read all the time. I didn't get many chances to read by not going to school, so when we went to the "Y" I could read some of the books that Ophilla could not buy for me. Even though I didn't go to school, my sister and brother-in-law and the Gates taught me to read, write, and count until I was as good as anyone in school.

I missed my friends in Cincinnati. We used to go to the park and play baseball in the summertime. Because I didn't go to school, I didn't get a chance to play with kids my age that often. When summer came and school was out for them, I would try to see them as much as possible. My girlfriends that went to school would talk about boys all the time. I didn't know too many boys, so they were not on my mind like my friends.

I first met Jimmy and Vi Owens in Cleveland. They had an after-hour spot near their home. I met them when they came to the Cedar Gardens to see me perform. They invited me to their club to entertain their guests. I agreed, and they advertised the show all over the town to pack the house. Many people who couldn't afford to go to the Cedar Gardens would come to their club and get to see me. Jimmy and Vi's club was one of the hottest after-hour clubs in Cleveland. The joint was always jumping.

After I performed at the Cedar Gardens, I would head straight for their club. I was always treated like a VIP by everyone and could always unwind at the club. Being around my people made me feel good after performing for primarily white people all the time. While I was working at the Cedar Gardens, I met Olympic Gold Medal winner, Jesse

Owens. He lived in Cleveland and had a dry-cleaning business. At first, I didn't know he was an award-winning athlete. Jesse traveled a lot, running in track meets all over the country and the world. But, when he was in Cleveland, he would always come by the club to see me perform.

I found out that Jesse had fallen for me by accident. I would send my clothes to the cleaners, and every time I got them back, there would be no charge. This went on for so long that I began to think something was strange. If I didn't get a bill soon, I wouldn't be able to pay for my clothes. One night after I performed, I was sitting with Jesse at his table talking. "Jesse, someone at the cleaners returned my clothes to me and did not send the bill."

He replied, "Oh, don't worry about the bill; I own the cleaners and told my employees not to charge you. I like you very much and wanted to do something for you."

Jesse and I became good friends. He took me out on several occasions, but we were always in different parts of the country because of our work commitments. When he was not running somewhere, he would follow me wherever I was performing. We never became intimate, as I was still involved with Louis Armstrong. And I would never mess around with two men at the same time. When Jesse was overseas, he would call me all the time, and he would tell me how his running was going, and I would tell him about my dancing and singing. He never stopped trying to get me.

Jesse was having a difficult time in those days. The U.S.A. had turned its back on Jesse. He was better received in Europe than his own country. You would think that a national hero that had done the impossible would have been treated better, but he was still a colored man in a white man's world.

After I left Cleveland, I went back to Chicago to work at the Grand Terrace Nightclub. I liked it there, it was such a fabulous club and the people in Chicago loved me. I had a strange thing happen to me one night. I was in between sets when Mr. Fox told me that I didn't have to do my next show. I asked him, "Why? I don't want to lose any money by not performing."

Mr. Fox said, "Trust me, you will still get paid. There is a gentleman who paid us to let someone else perform so that he can talk to you." I was very suspicious but I went to see this Mr. "X", a white man sitting in the audience. I made my way to him, and champagne and a white envelope was on the table. He invited me to sit down and told me how much he liked my performance. He said he had a club in New York City and when I finished my engagement at the Grand Terrace to come to New York and work for him. We talked for a while, and when we finished, he gave me his address and the envelope. Inside the envelope were several 100 dollar bills. He told me that he was serious and gave me an advance to show how earnest he was. I thought that it was strange, but I took the money and thanked him.

After finishing work at the Grand Terrace, I headed for New York. When I got there, I got a room and sent a message to the address given to me by "Mr. X". There was no response from the telegram, so I went to work at the Kit Kat Club. I thought it was strange for him to give me money to work for him, so I sent him another telegram. Late one night, after I had gotten off from work at the club, there was a knock at my door. It was two o'clock in the morning, and I was in my gown. I asked, "Who is it?"

"This is the police," a voice said.

"What do you want? I haven't done anything."

The voice said, "If you don't open the door, we will break it down!"

"Let me see your badges," I said as I put the chain on the door and cracked it to see their badges. Two men busted in the door and put a gun upside my head. I was scared to death and did not understand what was going on.

They gave me a telegram and asked, "Did you send this telegram?"

Frightened, I said, "Yes!" They asked me if I knew Mr. "X". I have to use Mr. "X" because I found out he was an international gangster. I told them about how we met and that he told me to get in touch with him when I got to New York. They started to search my room; they looked everywhere trying to find someone. I was afraid of these two men; I thought they were going to rape me. They told me that they would kill me if I ever tried to contact Mr. "X" again. They said that his wife got the telegram and wanted to know who I was. Mr. "X" told her he didn't know who I was and sent these two thugs to see me. They turned to each other, and one said to the other, "She's a cute little dish. Mr. "X" likes her type." Then they left.

I had never been so afraid in my life. I later found out that the man I met in the bar was actually "Mr. X's" brother-in-law trying to set him up with me. However, his wife got the telegram instead of him, and when he found out he had to get out of it the best way he could.

After that experience, I headed for Atlantic City. While working and trying to get the Mr. "X" experience behind me, I started to dislike one of the girls in the chorus line. Now I don't know why I didn't like her, but I didn't. She never said or did anything to me. But every time I would see her, I had it in my heart to hate her. She tried to stay away from me, but that was hard for her because I was the star of the show, and everything centered on me. She was a nice, sweet girl who everyone liked. She came to my rescue once, which made me change my mind about her and stopped hating her. I said to myself that I would never hate anyone again.

The show moved to another theater, and my costume was lost. I knew I couldn't go on that night without it and didn't know what to do. That girl that I hated so much went out of her way to make me a costume. She took a bra and G-string and dyed them in coffee for me, so I would have something on when I performed. It was the kindest thing someone could do for me at the time, and I stopped hating her after that. I felt that I probably hated her because of what happened to me in New York with the gangsters and had to take it out on someone.

Not too long after that, I left the country for the first time and went to Havana, Cuba, with the Harlem Scandal Show. We performed in a beautiful theatre named Alkazar. I never knew what that meant, but it had a beautiful sound to it. The Cuban women I encountered were stunning, and they thought I was Cuban. I did look like them. My skin was silky smooth with a golden tan, and my hair was jet-black. Cuban women had that golden tan look with long jet-black hair. I remember how hot it was down there. I had never been anywhere in the states that was that hot, and I grew up in the south.

Figure 5: Newspaper clipping of "Lady Lane" heading to Havana.

Opening night was very exciting for me. I had never been outside of the country, nor had I performed for a non-English speaking audience. Everyone around us spoke Spanish, so we had to have a translator with us at all times. The Cuban men flirted with me and I didn't even know what they were saying to me. When we opened that night, I looked out at the audience from the wing to see a packed house. One of the guys said that Premier Batista was in the audience and pointed him out to me. How about that, I thought to myself, the Premier of another country coming to see me.

Cuba is such a beautiful country, and I would like to come back here someday. The show ran for several weeks and I think every Cuban had come to see me dance. I decided to stay in Cuba after the show had finished. Cuba had beautiful beaches and trees, and I loved to ride a bike along the countryside. The people were very friendly, and the children were nice. When the show was here, the only problem we had was that the children would steal some food because they were hungry. There were a lot of poor people in Cuba. Batista was a dictator and kept the people in poverty. Many tourists came to Cuba in those days because it was a beautiful country and so close to the United States. After staying in Cuba for a while, I headed back to New York to see what I could get going. By now, I was over my fear of the gangsters and was ready to start working again. They were working on the movie "The Singing Kid," I wanted to do another film. The excitement is great, and you have a lot of fun.

Nina Mae McKinney was one of the top-colored stars of those days and I heard that this movie was to have an all-colored cast. The movie's name was "The Devil's Daughter" and filmed in Jamaica. The day I went to the casting, I was very nervous. I was trying out for a speaking part and one of the main characters in the movie. When I got to the casting office, there were many beautiful women there. Most of them knew me. By now, I was as famous as Nina Mae was. The casting director and the producer also knew me.

I was cast to play the role as a Jamaican girl, Elvira. Hamtree Harrington played a Harlem boy who went to Jamaica, and I became his girlfriend. Others cast for lead roles were Jack Carter, Ida James, Emmett "Babe" Wallace and Francine Larrimore. The night before we were to go to Jamaica, I could hardly sleep. The excitement of going to a beautiful country like Jamaica after just coming back from Cuba was overwhelming. Girl, I said to myself, this is your lucky moment; you are not just a cast member. You are one of the stars in this movie, and who knew where this would lead me to in my career.

That morning at the airport, I met some of the other cast members. The director and the producer were there with all the camera and technician men. Everybody was very excited about going to Jamaica. It would be our first time there for most of us, and many were leaving the United States for the first time.

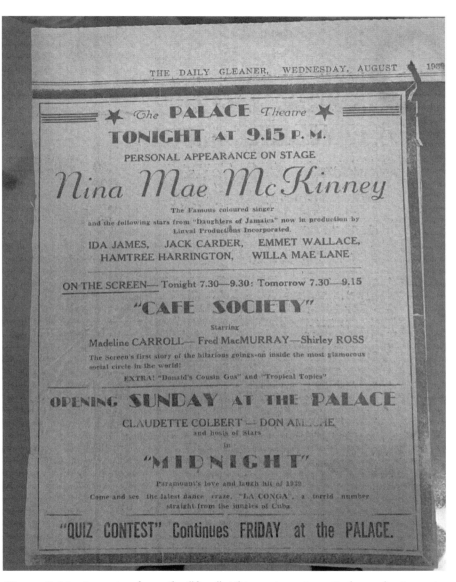

Figure 6: Movie poster from the "first" African American Independent movie.

Figure 7: The set in Kingston, Jamaica 1936 "The Devil's Daughter."

We were on the plane heading for Jamaica when we flew over Cuba. I thought about my stay there, and I was still very nervous about flying in airplanes. This was my second time going overseas. I sat in my seat thinking about my family. At this point, I was communicating with several of them. My brother Dolphus was the younger of my brothers, he had become very close to me. I would send him money when he needed it or a new coat that he had to have. Most of my brothers and sisters still didn't like me, but I didn't let that bother me. I was happy and my career was going very well, and I was on my way to make a movie that I would get a lot of recognition.

We landed in Kingston; it was as beautiful as Cuba with its beaches, palm trees, and flowers. The people were charming, and the climate was hotter than Cuba to me. There were a lot of poor people around begging for money, and that upset me very much. I had not seen this many poor colored people in all my life. We were not rich in Clayton, Alabama, and were considered poor like most sharecropping families. But we always had plenty of food. We raised pigs, cows, and chickens. These people had nothing and were begging in the streets like I had never seen before. Little dirty children would come up to me and ask for a penny. I wanted to cry at what I saw. Here I was in my fine clothes and money in my pocket and knowing that I would be going to the U.S. when I finished the movie and would have plenty of everything.

When we started shooting the movie "The Devil's Daughter," we were very excited. It was an all-colored cast with some well-known stars in it. The movie was about voodoo and how a boy from Harlem got caught up in it. We had a lot of colorful costumes and headpieces. My role was a Jamaican girl who became the girlfriend of this Harlem boy who came to Jamaica. My character in the movie walked barefooted. Oh, how I hated that! All my life, I despised going barefooted. When we shot the first of my scenes, we were in the woods, and something jumped on my shoulder. I hollered, ran out of the scene, and kept on running. This continued on happening as things kept jumping on my feet. The director sent me to town to buy me some sandals. That was the only way I would work in the woods, and most of the scenes were in the woods.

Things were going well in the movie. I wasn't as afraid as I was in the beginning and I could run through the woods saying, "Harlem boy where is you, Harlem boy where is you." I was a pretty Jamaican girl who fell in love with Harlem boy. Hamtree was a handsome man and all the girls were in love with him, but he was mine. After we finished the movie and headed back to the states, we had several press parties for the movie. Newspapers were writing stories and photographers were always taking our pictures. It was not like the other movie I was in; this time I expected to get a lot more offers to do films and headline other big events.

CHAPTER TEN
THE JOINT IS JUMPING

New York City, the 1940s. Now that I'm in the fast lane, the years have passed by so swiftly. My career was moving like no one would have ever believed. I will turn twenty-one years old this year and have been in show business for almost eight years. I have made some significant accomplishments in my life - fame and some fortune. I have everything a girl could want. No, I don't have everything! I still don't have a man to myself. I have Louis, but he is not all mine. I keep telling myself that when I find the right man, I will be through with Louis.

I started hanging around with the real swinger, Herman Henderson. Mr. Fletcher was writing music for me. Times were changing, and I started thinking about recording some of my music. Word was out that the record companies would start recording more colored women singers; very few were on records at this point in history. Swing was really in now. After Benny Morton died, Count Basie took over his band. During my time working at the Grand Terrace, I met Earl "Fatha" Hines and Fats Waller. These guys were the real swingers. Fats and I hung out on several occasions. If we went to a club to see someone else perform, they would ask him to do a number like they did every entertainer that stopped by. I would always be with him if I wasn't working and perform a number. Fats would get on the piano and play until he would fall out on the floor. I would get up there, do a dance and then do the chicken legs over him. The crowd would love it.

Fats and I had some great times together. He loved to give parties for people in show business. He would rent a suite and multiple rooms to throw a party whenever he was in the mood. One time, Fats had a party in Boston, and the place was rocking. I jumped up on the bed and hollered, "The Joint is Jumping!" Not too long after this party, Fats made a song with my saying, and the song became a big hit. Everybody knew he got that from me, but he never gave me a dime for it.

My birthday rolled around, and the club owner where I was working threw a party for me that evening after the show. Some of the entertainers in town came to my party. Some of the people that were in the audience at the show even stayed for the party. They had a big cake for me, and all my entertainer friends performed a number for me. My birthday party was the club's second show of the night. For many years, I did not celebrate my birthdays because I was always hiding my actual age. And when you work in show business, entertainers are always busy and on the road. We rarely got a chance to have a holiday off or enjoy a birthday. Holidays have always been big business for clubs and theaters. But this party turned out exactly how a birthday celebration should be: fun times with family and friends.

By now, I had performed just about everywhere and done almost everything. I was always looking for something different. I called my agent, Mrs. Hazel Green, to see if she had something unique for me. She told me to come downtown to her office on 42nd Street to see her. The World's Fair was in New York, and they were auditioning for a show in the fair.

At the time, I was living in Harlem at the Braddock Hotel on 8th Avenue. I took the subway downtown to see her. During the ride, I kept thinking if I could get a job at the fair, people from all over the world would see me perform. Wouldn't that be great? I thought, International Willa Mae Lane. I got goosebumps all over my body thinking about that type of notoriety. How exciting that would be!

Mrs. Green secured an audition appointment for me, and I went out to Flushing Meadows to see the show's producer, Mr. Gibbs. The show was in the Why Do Theater. There were a lot of girls there auditioning for the show. Most of them were white girls, but there were a few colored girls along with myself. I thought they would pick all white girls, but they chose me and another colored girl, Naomi.

Some of the shows at the Fair were outside on a big stage with a band backing them up; but the Why Do Theater was inside. We had records to dance by that Mr. Gibbs bought for us. Our show went on all season, whereas the shows outside would change.

We always had a great time doing the show. We had different performers every fifteen minutes in the theater, so you had to work all day from one o'clock until eleven. The whole show stopped for one hour for a dinner break. At that time, you could go and taste some of the foods from all over the world. After I had done that, I started bringing my lunch as the days were very long, and I needed time to relax.

It was an enjoyable job to have. I met a lot of people from all over the world, and they enjoyed my dancing. I did an African dance in a feather costume with Tom-tom drum music. There was another girl named Norma that did a Hindu dance. She was dressed up as an East Indian. One of the girls in the show had a half-man, half-woman costume. She would perform her number from each side of her outfit. She was one of the people from the show who stood outside the theater to attract people to the show. A barker would be telling everyone to go inside and see the show. They had a life-size color poster of me in a feathered costume. I was so glad I didn't have to stand out there like the other girls.

On my dinner break, I would go to the back of the theater and sit under a shade tree. I would sit and watch the ducks in the lake that was in the middle of the fair and think of all the good things that happened to me. Some of the girls would join me and we would talk and feed the birds. I enjoyed their company, especially if you wanted to take a nap, you had to make sure that someone would wake you up in time to get ready to do your show. Once our break was over, it was a steady grind, one show after another.

It was about eleven-thirty at night when we left the fairgrounds. I had one of the longest rides back to Harlem, but we all rode the subway together. I had to change trains three times, but I didn't have to worry about crime like you have to now. It was about one o'clock in the morning when I got to Harlem, and I was glad to be home.

The Three Rockets were also working at the fair at another theater. We would go and see each other's show, and when a big group of colored people would come to see us, we would really get down in our act.

When the fair was over that fall, I decided to take some time off. It had been a long season, and I needed a rest. I was in touch with my brother, Dolphus King, who lived in Johnstown, PA. I still didn't get along with all my brothers and sisters, which bothered me for a long time. Nevertheless, Dolphus was a sweet boy, and I loved him very much. If he needed anything and could not afford it, I wouldn't hesitate to buy it for him.

While taking time off, I would hang around the number holes in Harlem and play my numbers. Single action would keep me in the streets all day, waiting for the numbers to come out one by one. It was fun being out there with all the people hanging around. You could go into the corner drugstore and have a fountain soda or go into the shoeshine parlor and shoot the fat with the boys. Harlem was exciting in those days, but it started to change. More and more colored people were moving into Harlem, and the whites were moving out. Drugs were beginning to take hold in the neighborhood, and people's lives were being destroyed. Little did I know it would still be going on today.

After my short break ended, I decided to take a gig in Atlantic City at Club Harlem; it was a Las Vegas show club. They had a chorus line, a big band, and a comedian to support the acts. When you entered the club, they gave you a pair of wooden knockers. You did not clap for the entertainers; you hit the knockers on the table. It was exciting and a lot of fun.

When I returned to New York City, I started hanging out with the swingers again. They named me "The Queen of Swing." Earl Garner had a club on 42nd Street where all the entertainers hung out. Peggy Lee and Billie Holiday would be there a lot when they were in town. And Dinah Washington would come around from time to time. All the big band leaders like Duke, Count, and Louis would also hang. The forties seemed to change the way music was being played.

DINAH WASHINGTON

UNIVERSAL ATTRACTIONS
2 Park Avenue New York 16, N. Y.

Figure 8: The Great Dinah Washington known for her song
"What a Difference a Day Makes."

Big clubs in the north started to open their doors to colored people if they had the money. Time was still hard for most post the Great Depression, but you would see a few in the audience from time to time. Most colored people liked to go to the colored joints and be with their own people. And trust me, the colored joints were jumping all the time.

I wanted to dance at Smalls Paradise once. It was the biggest club in Harlem and was always jumping. The people would pack the place, and the cars would be double and triple parked outside. I went to see about a job there, and the show producer told me that I had to audition. Can you believe that he wanted me, Willa Mae Lane - International star, to audition? And this turkey knew my reputation to pack a club out, and he still told me, "you have to audition." I told him I had worked bigger and better clubs than Smalls Paradise, and I wouldn't audition for him at any time. I never wanted to work there after that, although I would go there at times as a patron.

Within days of that incident, I got a job at the Club Reno in Saratoga, New York. Max Baer, world heavyweight champion, was the owner. Max was a big-time gambler. The night I started working, he sent roses to pay his respect. It was a classy club with a rather large dance floor and stage. One waiter made all the entertainers mad all the time. Instead of walking around the dance floor as the other waiters did, he would cut across the dance floor while we were performing. No matter how irritated he made the patrons, he continued to do it. So, I told the manager to ask him not to cross the dance floor while I was performing. But he didn't seem to care and continued to walk across the stage in front of me.

One night I decided to fix him. I waited until his tray was loaded with drinks. I was doing my dance routine and was looking for him out the corner of my eye. Then I saw him, his tray was loaded with Champagne and wine and he walked in front of me. I did one of my high kicks and kicked onto the floor, and I kept on dancing like nothing even happened. He got down on his hands and knees to clean up the mess. Boy, oh boy was he mad, but I didn't care. I told him not to walk in front of me. The manager came over and told him he would have to pay for that tray of drinks; it was about fifty dollars. The waiter had the nerve to ask me to pay for it, and I told him I wouldn't pay for anything. I had asked him not to walk in front of me and besides I didn't see him, is what I told him. From that time on, he never walked across the dance floor again.

Life was great for me in those days; everything I touched turned to gold. My movie, "The Devil's Daughter," was out, but somehow, I was too busy to see it. After working at Club Reno, I decided to go back to Buffalo, New York to work. It had been several years since I worked there, and they had many clubs for me to choose from. The forties were the swinging years, and a club didn't have to be in a major city. There were a lot of clubs in small cities and towns that drew people from all over.

I left Saratoga and went back to Harlem to prepare for my trip to Buffalo. When I finished with my contract in Buffalo, my mind was made up; I was determined to start my recording career. I loved to sing and dance, but dancing was something that I did on stage to be enjoyed at the moment. Singing was something I wanted to do so people could enjoy my songs all the time.

CHAPTER ELEVEN
NIGHTMARE

It was late August when I arrived in Buffalo. The city was still hot and humid. Most of the streets seem deserted since the school was still out. The University of Buffalo and all its students made up a large part of Buffalo. I got a room at the Verdon Hotel, and when I was settled in, I decided to look around town to see what had changed. It did not seem like it was several years ago since I was there last. I walked over to the Little Harlem Club, where I performed during my last stay. Boy, I would not mind performing here again. I had a lot of fun and met some friendly people there. Oh well, I will go over to the Club Moonglow to see what it looks like.

When I got to Club Moonglow, it was still jumping! I asked one of the people cleaning up where I could find Mr. Levy, the owner. He looked up at me and said, "You are Willa Mae Lane? I have seen you before, and I think you are great."

"Thank You." He showed me to Mr. Levy's office. Before I knocked on his door, I tugged on my clothes to make sure they were in order; I liked to look my best at all times. I knocked, and a voice said, "Come in." I went in and saw a pleasant-looking man sitting behind his desk looking over some papers. Before I could say anything, he said, "Willa Mae Lane, you look beautiful. You are everything they said about you. I am Max Levy, and it's a pleasure to meet you."

"Thank you," I said to him as I took his hand that he extended to me.

"I think you will like my club, we have a great staff of people and an excellent clientele of people that come here. You are well-known all over the country for your great dancing and singing. And it is an honor to have you at my club. Do you mind if I show you around? After that, you can meet the boys in the band and rehearse your numbers with them."

I was impressed by his introduction and thanked him for his words. He took me around, showing me the changes the club had made since my last visit. When we got to the stage, I looked out and imagined it was filled to capacity. I played at so many clubs and theaters, but this one felt good to be in.

After I finished rehearsing, I said goodbye to everyone. I decided I would walk around the neighborhood to see what was there. It was a warm afternoon as I left the club and walked toward my hotel. I stopped and looked into several store windows. There was a drug store with a soda fountain in it. During that time, most of the drug stores had soda fountains and ice cream parlors in them. Oh, wouldn't it be nice to stop and have an ice cream sundae, I thought as I walked by.

Then I passed a hardware store with abundant garden supplies, buckets of nails, and screws in the window. I continued to walk, thinking about my opening night at the club, and before I knew it, I was back at the hotel.

That night at my opening, I felt a little nervous, but I always felt a little nervous before I opened, but once I am out on the stage, I am in my own world. I loved to dance, sing, and make people feel good. I didn't sing too many songs that made you feel sad and blue. Most of my tunes made you feel good. And I did lively dance numbers that would keep your feet patting and your hands clapping. It was finally my turn. I walked onto the stage and started to sing a song. The people were feeling that song when suddenly the music changed, and I began dancing. I danced until I knew the crowd was loving me. They were shouting and clapping their hands and having such a good time that I did not want to stop. When I did, they kept on hollering for more. That was a great opening night for me.

A few days later, Mr. Levy had a bigger-than-life picture billboard of me made and put on top of the club. At night when it was all lit up, you could see it for miles. He wanted everyone in Buffalo to know that Willa Mae Lane was here. Mr. Levy was a good man and liked me very much, his wife was a beautiful woman, and we got along fine.

There was another showgirl, Suzy Brown, that people thought looked like me and would get us confused at times. But there was only one Willa Mae Lane. I was the greatest and one of the country's most famous showgirls, known by everybody in show business. Life was great for me, and I couldn't think of anything that could hold me back from becoming a successful recording star. Several other colored women were recording stars, and now it was my turn to record music. Most of the girls could only sing; however, I was a great dancer and singer. But when the door of recording music opened up for colored women, I was not one of the first to go in. I took my time because my career was going so well. I promised myself that as soon as I got back to New York City, I would start recording.

One night as I was in my dressing room, I noticed that a couple of light bulbs were out around the mirror. I recalled the hardware store that I came across on my first night in town. I reminded myself to stop by there tomorrow on my way to work and pick up a couple of light bulbs. After all, I had to look good at all times and didn't want to miss anything by not having good lighting. I laughed about it as I prepared to go home.

We had worked through Labor Day. With the summer over and school getting ready to start in a week, I didn't want to shop anywhere as the stores would be filled with college students buying all the things they needed.

Morning came with the sun shining brightly in my room—what a beautiful morning. I went to the window and looked out. Buffalo was a small yet beautiful city. I looked at the calendar; it was September 6th, and Autumn set in pretty fast in Buffalo. I decided to take my bath, get dressed, and go out into this beautiful day before heading to the club for my afternoon rehearsal. I wanted to get something to eat and get some exercise to keep my body in shape. With all the dancing I do, you wouldn't think that I would need any more activity, but I had to keep my body toned at all times. I moved swiftly through the day, and rehearsal went great. I wanted to get back to my room and take a bath a little early, so I could get ready to leave in time to stop by the hardware store and pick up some light bulbs for my dressing room. It was a little past nine when I left my room to go to the hardware store. I walked up to Williams Avenue to the store and saw three little children playing in the street. I went into the store and got the light bulbs I needed. When I left, the children were still out there riding a tricycle. I stopped and asked them, "What are you all doing out so late?"

They answered, "Just out riding."

"It was very late, and I wouldn't want anything to happen to you. Does your mother know where you are?"

"No," one boy said, "we are all right. You sure are pretty, lady! What's your name?"

"You wouldn't know, but your mother might. My name is Willa Mae Lane. They call me "Lady Lane."

One of the boys replied shyly, "You sure are pretty. Would you buy us some ice cream, please?"

"I will tell you what; I will buy you all some ice cream, but only if you promise to go straight home and not stop anywhere else."

They all replied in unison, "We will!"

I fished around my purse for some change, and then we went into the drug store to get them some ice cream. As we left the store, I told them, "Now I want you to go straight home, and maybe I will see you again sometime."

They all thanked me and started to ride their tricycle down the street. The three children got several feet away from me when I heard someone come up behind me. I turned and saw a woman, and before I could say or do anything, she smashed a glass of something into my face. The cup broke, cut my forehead, and I began to feel a warm sensation over my face. "Hey, what are you doing to me?" I screamed as she turned and ran down the street. All of a sudden, my face was on fire. I screamed out in pain, "Help me, somebody help me, please, help me!" I continued to scream as I felt my skin melting off my face. "Oh God, my skin is melting off my face. God, what has happened to me?" People started coming from everywhere to help me.

"It is Lady Lane," someone said, "something happened to Lady Lane." I was lying on the ground when Cooky and others who worked at the club came over to help me. I was screaming, "Help me, please!"

Cooky, the headwaiter, said, "Sugar, let me help you get into the club." Everyone helped me off the ground and across the street to Club Moonglow.

"This looks very bad," Cooky said. They put some cold water on my face and butter on my skin, for they didn't know what to do. They called an ambulance and the fire department. People were everywhere inside the club and outside in the street. Everybody wanted to know what had happened to Lady Lane.

When the ambulance came, they looked at me and said, "This is very bad; we better take her to the hospital right now." They put me in the ambulance and drove me to the hospital. Cooky went with me. They took me to Mother Cabrini Hospital. When I got to the hospital, they put me in a room in the emergency section. A doctor came in and looked at my face and chest. I heard him tell somebody that it looked terrible. He told them to get something, and a few minutes later, they put something on my face. It was thick and greasy, but it cooled my face instantly. I heard them talking some more. They were asking Cooky who I was and whether I had money, insurance, or family that could take care of the bill. Cooky told them that he didn't know too much about me because I had just got there a couple of weeks ago.

I laid there in extreme pain, and all they could think about was who was going to pay the bill? I continuously cried out for help, but no one helped me. I tossed and turned, trying not to pass out, but the pain was more than I could bear. I wanted to tear my skin off in the hopes of getting some relief. No one came, no one helped. I felt like my whole body was on fire, and someone tried to put it out with more fire. The more it burned, the more fire was being used. I screamed as loud as I could, "Lord Jesus, help me! Why is this happening to me? Who did this to me?"

Cooky came back into the room and said, "I have to go back to the club but don't worry, everything is going to be all right." He took my hand and held it tight.

I whispered to him, "Cooky, I can't see, please don't leave me, please don't leave. I am so afraid."

He reassured me, "Everything is going to be all right; they will take care of you." He started to leave, but I would not let his hand go. I held on for dear life because I knew that I was all alone and had no one. "Now, Sugar," he said in a soft, loving tone, "I got to go, but someone will be here soon." With that, I reluctantly released his hand and pleaded with him not to go. He said, "don't worry, just rest." And then the door opened and closed. I was alone again.

After Cooky left, I laid there in terrible pain, wondering when someone would come in and do something to help me. Oh God, am I going to die? Is this as bad as they say? Will I be blind? All these thoughts raced through my mind. Why won't they do something? "Help!" I screamed, "Help me, please!"

I must have passed out for a minute. When I woke up, someone was standing over me, asking questions that I didn't understand. The pain numbed my body and mind until I didn't know what they were asking or what I was saying. All I knew was that my face was on fire, and I needed immediate relief. Finally, I began to hear a voice faintly saying, "We can't do anything at this time; we are waiting to get some information on you." He looked at my face and commented that the burns were severe. He told me, "It appears that you have lost sight in your left eye."

"Oh, no! Oh, no! Oh, no!" I cried out. "Oh God, please help me."

The doctor left; again, I was alone in a strange place with half my face eaten away and blind in one eye, and no one will help me. What kind of world do we live in? It was late, but how late I didn't know. I could hear people outside my room talking, and some of it was about me. I got mad, but what could I do? I couldn't go anywhere, nor could I see. What am I going to do?

"Willa, it is me, Max, Max Levy."

"Oh, Mr. Levy, please help me. They will not do anything to help me; please make them do something." I cried, but there were no tears.

"Mrs. Levy is here with me, and we are going to do everything we can. We will make sure they take good care of you here until we transfer you somewhere else for specialty care. I am going to talk to the doctor and find out what he is going to do. We will be right back."

"Please don't leave me, Mr. Levy," I cried out.

But I was grateful to him for coming to see about me. Oh, thank you, God, for sending me someone like Mr. Levy. I don't know what I would have done if someone had not cared. As I laid in this bed, it felt like I was spinning around and around. I grabbed the rails to keep from falling off the bed, but I wasn't moving. It was just my mind. "Mr. Levy, please come back," I mumbled, "please come back." Then I passed out again.

I woke up in what seemed to be hours later. The room was still dark, but I could hear Mr. Levy talking. "Willa, we are trying to make some arrangements to move you to another hospital. This one seems to think you can't pay your bill if they treat you. So, I told them they were not the only hospital in town and we would find another one that will take care of you. After all, you are the great Willa Mae Lane, one of the most beautiful entertainers in the country. Now you just lay there, and we'll be back in a moment and get you out of here." They left again. But this time, I knew that I was not alone.

Mr. Levy's words kept replaying in my mind. "After all, you are the great Willa Mae Lane, one of the most beautiful entertainers in the country." But am I still beautiful? What do I look like? Everyone keeps saying it looks very bad. I wanted to see just how bad it was. What if I lose my sight in my right eye and never see again? Oh, Jesus, save my right eye; please let me see again.

"Lady Lane," I was startled by the voice.

"Who is it?"

"It is me, Jimmy Owen."

"Is that really you, Jimmy?"

"Yes, and Vi is here too."

I sighed sincerely, "Oh, thank God somebody is here that is not going to leave me. This has been a nightmare, Jimmy. I have been here all night, and all they tell me is we can't do anything for you now. Vi, look at my face and tell me what I look like. I have to know. Please, Vi!"

"There is ointment all over your face, so it is hard to tell, but you have been burned very badly," she said. I could hear the concern in her voice.

"Am I blind? Am I ugly? Vi, please tell me the truth. I am ugly, ain't I?"

"No, you are not ugly, just burned, and they can fix that, I know they can. Everything will be alright; just you wait and see." Although she was trying to comfort me, I could hear the fear in her tone.

I hesitated before I spoke but then blurted out, "But I can't see Vi, I can't see. I don't want to live if I can't see and if I am ugly. I just want to die."

"You can't mean that," said Jimmy. "What about all your friends? What about us? We all love you and need you. We want you to live so you can dance again and sing to us. Now stop talking about dying. You will live to be an old, beautiful lady."

Mr. Levy came back in and said, "Willa, it's all set; we are moving you to the finest hospital in Buffalo, the Millard Fillmore Hospital." I was a bit shocked by this news.

"Mr. Levy, from what I hear, they don't let colored people in that hospital." At that moment, Mr. Levy grabbed my hand and said, "Listen, when Max Levy says the Millard Fillmore, he means the Millard Fillmore. Trust me, ok? And who are your visitors here?"

"This is Jimmy Owens and his wife Vi; they are friends of mine from Cleveland. Jimmy and Vi, this is my boss, Mr. Levy."

"Pleased to meet you," they all say to each other.

After a moment, Mr. Levy grabs both of my hands and reassures me, "I will be back. I am going to arrange to have an ambulance to take you straight to Millard Fillmore Hospital. I will be back."

"Oh, thank you, Mr. Levy, thank you."

After he left, I reached my hand out for Jimmy and Vi. They both took a hand. I told them, "I am so afraid to go to that hospital by myself after what I have been through here. Will you go with me?"

"Of course we will," they said.

Jimmy squeezed my hand tighter and said, "We are not going to leave you, Brown Sugar; we will do everything that we can to help you; this is my promise to you."

"Yes," echoed Vi. "Now, let's get you ready to get out of this place they call a hospital."

The ambulance came, and we left for the Millard Fillmore. During the ride to the hospital, I felt that maybe things just might be okay for the first time since the incident occurred.

Several hospital staff members were waiting for me when we arrived at Millard Fillmore. They assigned me to a suite with a living room and a bed. Dr. Haig was the first doctor who came to speak to me. He told me that my right eye could be saved. Thank God! He also said that after my skin healed and the swelling goes down, they could tell me more about the damage. I was still covered with bandages, so I couldn't tell what I looked like.

Flowers, cards, telegrams, and money started coming in from all over the country. People who I didn't know sent me things. It was a great feeling to know that people cared about me. Jimmy and Vi stayed a couple of days until my sister, Ella, arrived. I hated to see them go, but I knew they couldn't stay forever. I was so thankful for them, for I was lost without someone that I knew. A few weeks later, Mr. Levy brought in one of the best plastic surgeons in the country, Dr. Brown, to see me. After studying and examining my face, he told me, "When I finish, you will be as beautiful as before, and no one will know the difference." It was a long, drawn-out process. He took skin from my legs and grafted it into my face. He made me a new eyelid for my left eye, took hair from my body, and made eyebrows. I was blind in my left eye, but he did not remove the eye. He let it remain so that it would keep its shape. Dr. Brown did a beautiful job on my face, and as he promised me, in the end, no one could tell that my face was burned with lye. It was a miracle operation for this was in 1942.

After several weeks, I was released from the hospital to go home. In all that time, I never talked to a psychiatrist or a social worker about my mental state of mind. They just released me after they put the outside of me back together. But what about the inside of me that was severely damaged? This terrible incident constantly stayed on my mind. I had ongoing nightmares about it. They were so vivid; I felt like I was reliving each moment. I had a hard time sleeping, and I was very jumpy. I would hear noises when there was no noise and see things when there was nothing. My mind was a wreck, and my nerves were shot. I took treatment for my eye for several weeks after my release from the hospital. I wanted to go back to work, back on stage where I belonged. I prayed to God to let me go back to work. As a child, I wanted to be in show business; there was nothing else I wanted to do. I asked God to show me the way, show me how I could go back to work, show me how to get back to my life of singing and dancing.

I spent many moments thinking about the woman that threw the lye on me. Eventually, I was told that the woman was looking for Suzy Brown, another showgirl working in Buffalo. She did look a lot like me and was supposedly seeing another woman's man. And my attacker threatened to do something to Suzy if she didn't stop seeing her man. The night she attacked me, she was actually looking for Suzy Brown, and I happened to be there, in the wrong place at the wrong time. Suzy

Brown came to visit me later and said she was not messing with anyone's man. But I didn't know one way or the other what she was doing.

When I was in the hospital, two white police officers came by my bedside and asked if I had any enemies in town. It was rumored that they found out who my attacker was and paid her to leave town. Buffalo was a close-knit town, and I knew they wouldn't tell me who she was. After I was recovered more, the same two police officers took me downtown to the police station to talk to a witness. The witness was a young man who said he saw the whole incident. He tried to describe the woman to the police officers and me. All he could tell us was that she was colored with dark skin and protruding teeth, but he didn't know who she was. The woman got away, and the police never looked too hard to find her. To this day, she has never come forward.

My recurring dream of flying in the air in a feather costume let me know that someday I would be back in show business dancing and singing. For me, it was important to show the public that nothing could stop Willa Mae Lane, the Queen of Swing, from doing what she loved. The woman who did this to me would have to live with what she did to me.

After a while, I met with Mr. Levy to ask him if I could come back to work once the doctor approved me. He told me that he would make me the manager of his club until I thought I was ready to perform again. By not working for such a long time and having so many hospital bills, I was in debt up to my ears. So, I was grateful that people and friends from all over the country were sending me money to help pay my bills.

CHAPTER TWELVE
HARLEM KNIGHT

Not too long after the attack, I met Harvey Whited. He was a debonair man - tall, confident, and knew exactly what he wanted in life. In the winter, he would wear his Chesterfield overcoats with the velvet collar, scarf, and a matching Fedora hat. He was always sharp. Not only was Harvey handsome and well dressed; but also, he was my "Harlem Knight" in shining armor.

After getting to know one another, Harvey started managing my career. Together we traveled the country, from LA to New York City. From Cotton Club to Cotton Club and all the rest in between. He managed my act well. I could clearly see that he was the right person for me. After the attack, I felt scared at times, not sure if something like that would happen again. While working with him on the road, he became my safe place, my shelter. Harvey stood a little over 6 feet tall and was about 212 pounds. He had a pleasant demeanor, but you didn't want to make him mad.

After coming off the road, we decided to settle in Harlem. Lenox Ave then to Seventh Ave in a small cold water flat. We loved Harlem even though it was overcrowded. My good friend Billie Holiday lived around the corner on Seventh Avenue. Over the years, Billie and I would hang around together – singing dancing and trading stories about our careers. In 1945, we moved to a well-known part of Harlem, "Sugar Hill". Sugar Hill was the upscale part of Harlem. The streets were so clean; some would say that you could almost eat off them. And our home was roomy and beautiful. Harvey was so proud of my career as an entertainer that he created a show room in the house where he displayed newspaper articles about me, my old show and movie posters, and professional portraits of me taken throughout the years.

Several years had passed since the attack, but I was still shaken on the inside. Over our 48-year marriage, Harvey proved to be someone that I could lean on and find comfort when those dark memories would haunt me. But the one event, that surpasses them all and helped bring healing was the birth of my son, Harvey Jr. He became my new focus in life, so much so that I retired from the show biz and became a housewife. All and all we had a good life, up on the "Hill." I was retired, but I would still dance at home to maintain my figure and my health. However, it was not the same. Deep down, I missed my entertainment life. Nevertheless, there was nothing that could tear me away from being a wife and mother to my Harveys.

As the "Queen of Swing", I experienced many highs and lows. At a young age, I escaped my familial fate of working in the cotton fields and/or as a cook or maid. I dreamed of becoming a famous dancer and through perseverance and pain, I achieved that dream and so much more. At 13, I charmed my way into an adult world. My beauty, natural-born talent, and vivid personality got me through multiple club doors. However, it was my confidence, strength, and belief in myself that continued to make me a sought-after entertainer from coast to coast. And being a black performer wasn't all pie in the sky. I had to fight for my position and for the will to remain in the industry. It took a lot of heart to become an entertainer at such a young age. Equally, it took a lot of heart to fight and change Jim Crow laws. But as my mother used to say, "Where there's a will, there is a way." I lived a great life – even with the ebbs and flows – they made me into an amazing woman, wife, and mother.

DEDICATED TO SWEET ELLA

My aunt, Ella Williams, and one of my mother's oldest sisters was commonly known as Aunt "Sweetie". She passed in 1978 at the age of 89 years old. Oh, how we loved Aunt Sweetie.

Ella was a shining light in the family. Aunt Ella was married to Mr. Bill Williams and they had a beautiful home. He was great too. But most of all we loved Ella because she was the one that went to her father, Daddy Ben King, and mother, Ella King, in protest of the criminal actions of this outlandish white person that tried to capture and rape my mother, Willa Mae.

Sister Ella King would not stand for these actions and she received permission to take Willa Mae up north to Ohio where she stepped off her world-famous career to stardom. May she always be cherished, loved, and admired. May she rest in peace.

INDEX